Lonely planet

D0556266

Pocket
MADEIRA
TOP EXPERIENCES · LOCAL LIFE · MADE EASY

Marc Di Duca

In This Book

QuickStart Guide

Your keys to understanding the island – we help you decide what to do and how to do it

Need to Know
Tips for a smooth trip

Regions
What's where

Explore Madeira

The best things to see and do, region by region

Top Experiences
Make the most of your visit

Local Life
The insider's island

The Best of Madeira

The island's highlights in handy lists to help you plan

Best Walks
See the island on foot

Madeira's Best...
The best experiences

Survival Guide

Tips and tricks for a seamless, hassle-free experience

Getting Around
Travel like a local

Essential Information
Including where to stay

Our selection of the island's best places to eat, drink and experience:

◉ **Experiences**

✖ **Eating**

🍷 **Drinking**

★ **Entertainment**

🔒 **Shopping**

These symbols give you the vital information for each listing:

📞 Telephone Numbers	👪 Family-Friendly
🕑 Opening Hours	🐾 Pet-Friendly
🅿 Parking	🚌 Bus
🚭 Nonsmoking	🚢 Ferry
@ Internet Access	Ⓜ Metro
🛜 Wi-Fi Access	Ⓢ Subway
🥗 Vegetarian Selection	🚊 Tram
🍴 English-Language Menu	🚆 Train

Find each listing quickly on maps for each region:

Bar Hemingway

16 🍷 Map p233, B2

Legend has it that Hemi self, wielding a machine rate this timber-pan tered bar during showpiece is a en by Papa ar town. Dress s.com; Hôtel Rit ; 🕑6.30pm-2a

6 ◉ Plac
V

QuickStart Guide 7

Madeira Top Experiences.....8

Madeira Local Life.............12

Madeira Day Planner.........14

Need to Know...................16

Madeira Regions.............18

Explore Madeira 21

22 West Funchal

48 East Funchal

72 North Coast

80 East Madeira

98 West Madeira

104 Mountains of the Interior

Worth a Trip:

Monte 68

Drive through
Eastern Madeira 78

Levada Paths 88

Porto Santo 112

The Best of Madeira 117

Madeira's Best Walks

Pico do Arieiro to Pico Ruivo **118**

Boca da Corrida to Encumeada **120**

Ponta de São Lourenço **122**

Madeira's Best...

Eating **124**

Drinking & Nightlife **126**

Shopping **127**

Museums & Galleries **128**

Tours **129**

For Kids **130**

Festivals & Events **131**

Beaches & Sea Swimming **132**

Villages **133**

For Free **134**

Wine Tasting **135**

Parks & Gardens **136**

Survival Guide 137

Before You Go **138**

Arriving in Madeira **139**

Getting Around **140**

Essential Information **142**

Language **145**

QuickStart Guide

Madeira Top Experiences 8

Madeira Local Life 12

Madeira Day Planner 14

Need to Know 16

Madeira Regions 18

Welcome to Madeira

Geologically dramatic, bursting with exotic colour and warmed year-round by the Atlantic sun, Portugal's most enchanting island is a place that keeps all its subtropical holiday promises. Pearl of the Atlantic, island of eternal spring...Madeira well deserves its fanciful nicknames and the affection visitors and locals alike feel for this tiny volcanic island that offers so much.

Funchal, viewed from the battlements of Fortaleza do Pico (p38)
PAUL BERNHARDT/GETTY IMAGES ©

Madeira Top Experiences

Zona Velha (p50)

Once a neglected ramshackle neighbourhood, Funchal's 'Old Zone' has been transformed into a characterful nightlife hotspot by imaginative bars and restaurants.

Monte (p68)

Climb aboard the cable car for a vertigo-inducing ascent to this cool, leafy neighbourhood of aristocratic villas gathered around Madeira's finest church. Make a swift descent in a wicker toboggan!

Quinta das Cruzes Museum (p24)

See how Madeira's other half once lived at this elegant mansion house museum documenting the lifestyles of Madeira's wealthy merchant classes and other notables of yesteryear.

Curral das Freiras (p106)

Make the gripping descent from Eira do Serrado along an ancient path down to this dramatically located village overhung on all sides by towering walls of rock.

Mercado dos Lavradores (p52)

Funchal's unmissable market is a riot of local sun-ripened colour and a place that gathers together the exotic produce Madeirans pluck from the generous Atlantic and harvest from their fertile volcanic soil.

Porto Santo (p112)

Madeira's little sister island may be a mere 14km long but it packs in several world-class attractions, most notably its alluring golden sands and a Ballesteros-designed golf course.

Jardins Botânicos da Madeira (p54)

Find out why Madeira is known as the island of eternal spring at these sloping gardens set high above Funchal, some of the finest in the world.

Museu de Arte Sacra (p26)

Admire the Flemish art and other religious works imported to Madeira between the 17th and 19th centuries by rich merchants and wealthy church institutions.

Sé (p28)

Madeira's top church was once the cathedral for the world's largest diocese and still exudes an air of ecclesiastic pomp.

Camacha Wicker Factory (p82)

Watch the local basket weavers at work at Camacha's O Relógio wicker factory where you can admire bizarre creations crafted from the humble willow wand.

Madeira Local Life

Insider tips to help you find the real Madeir

For a different perspective on Madeira, here's how you can experience what makes the island tick – the hidden gardens, black-sand beaches, amazing vistas and steep mountain roads that make Madeira for the Madeirans and tourists alike.

Wander along Frente Mar (p30)

▶ Ocean views
▶ Atlantic swimming

This sun-drenched amble runs along the Hotel Zone's stretch of coastline, where alongside the town's best places to stay, you'll find local kids playing football, bathing complexes, hidden swimming spots and viewpoints, and the long expanse of black sand that is Praia Formosa.

Explore São Martinho (p32)

▶ Quiet gardens and parks
▶ Panoramic vistas

Home to one in four Funchalese, wander through Funchal's suburbs to enjoy several verdant parks and gardens that the tourists seldom find. Stop off along the way for a *bica* (espresso) and a *pastel de nata* (custard tart) in one of many owner-run cafes.

Drive through Eastern Madeira (p78)

▶ Fascinating villages
▶ Dramatic views

Follow this winding rout through the island's east, making halts at mountai peaks, sandy beaches, a cliff-hugging swimming complex and Madeira's second 'city', Machico, en route. The going is steep, so practise those hill starts!

Igreja de São Martinho (p33)

Picnic facilities at a scenic lookout

Other great places to get a taste of local life in Madeira:

Ronaldo's statue (p37)

Saudade Madeira (p46)

Venda da Donna Maria (p61)

Armazém do Mercado (p64)

Santana's A-frame houses (p76)

Ponta do Pargo (p102)

Paúl da Serra (p111)

Madeira Day Planner

Day One

Your first port of call on any trip to Madeira should be Funchal town. You might want to start at the **Madeira Film Experience** (p36) for an easily digestible overview of the island's history. Popping into Madeira's cathedral, the **Sé** (p28), along the way, next stop should be the **Quinta das Cruzes Museum** (p24), where the life of the wealthy from centuries gone by comes under scrutiny.

After lunch take a stroll through the **Zona Velha** (p50) ending up at the cable-car station. Climb aboard for a glide above the rooftops of Funchal and into the clouds where the leafy neighbourhood of Monte is concealed 500m up. Visit the **Igreja da Nossa Senhora** (p69), have a coffee on romantic Largo da Fonte then take one of the famous toboggans back into the city.

If you have the evening to enjoy, take a stroll along the **Frente Mar** (p30), winding up at the black sand of **Praia Formosa** (p132) to watch the sensational Atlantic sunset ignite the horizon. Treat yourself to a seafood dinner at **Doca do Cavacas** (p31).

Day Two

Start the day exploring Madeira's astounding wealth of plant life at the **Jardins Botânicos da Madeira** (p54), a short bus ride from Funchal city centre. The cafe there is a superb place for lunch as you enjoy the views of Funchal and its bay.

Lunch with a view digested, head down to Praça do Município, Funchal's prettiest square where you can admire the surrounding basalt architecture as you wait for the **Museu de Arte Sacra** (p26) to reopen after the lunch break. Having admired the island's collection of priceless Flemish masters, next visit the quirkier gathering of objets d'art at the intriguing **Casa Museu Frederico de Freitas** (p36) nearby.

Some of Funchal's best eating options are in the Zona Velha. For authentic Madeiran fare from the backstreets of Funchal take a seat at **Venda da Donna Maria** (p61). For seafood in the company of the rich and famous try **Gaviã Novo** (p59). Dinner can be followed up with a few ponchas (sugar-cane alcohol) at **Mercearia da Poncha** (p62) or cocktails at **Barreirinha Cafe** (p62).

Short on time?

We've arranged Madeira's must-sees into these day-by-day itineraries to make sure you see the very best of the island in the time you have available.

Day Three

☀ You have to hit the **Mercado dos Lavradores** (p52) early to see the fish market in full flow. Having come face-to-face with the scary scabbard fish, you might be in need of a restorative coffee-and-cake halt at nearby **Pau de Canela** (p62), an authentically cheap Funchal cafe. Nearby, make sure you don't miss the **Armazém do Mercado** (p64) with its local food, hip eateries, pop-up stalls and toy museum.

☀ It's time to leave the city and head for the fishing village of **Câmara de Lobos** (p102) to the west of Funchal. After a *poncha* with the local fisherfolk, clamber aboard the tourist train that runs from here to **Cabo Girão** (p101), a sea cliff measuring 580m with a glass observation deck suspended over the abyss.

☽ If you time things right or take a taxi, you can enjoy dinner and fiery Macaronesian sunset back in Câmara de Lobos. **Vila do Peixe** (p102) specialises in grilled fish, **Vila da Carne** (p103) is the place to try *espetada* – seasoned grilled beef on a skewer.

Day Four

☀ Time to strike out into the wilds with a hire-car tour of some of the island's best sights. Head north out of Funchal early enough to catch the sunrise from the top of **Pico do Arieiro** (p109), Madeira's third-highest mountain, with a road leading to the summit. From there it's a short drive to chilly Ribeiro Frio with its **Balcões** (p109) viewpoint and **trout farm** (p110). Enjoy one of the latter's inhabitants at the cosy **Restaurante Ribeiro Frio** (p111).

☀ Descend to the north coast for a short stop off in Santana to check out the local thatched **A-frame houses** (p76). Continue west along the north coast to São Vicente for a guided tour of the **Grutas e Centro do Vulcanismo** (p75). The drive back to the south coast takes you through the mammoth valley that divides the island in two, a truly memorable experience.

☽ The central valley deposits you at the pretty town of Ribeira Brava, where you can enjoy dinner with sea views at **Borda D'Agua** (p103) or **Muralha** (p103). From here it's a short trip along the Via Rápida back to Funchal.

Need to Know

For more information, see Survival Guide (p137)

Currency
Euro (€)

Languages
Portuguese, English

Visas
Not required for nationals of most countries.

Money
ATMs widely available. Credit cards accepted in the vast majority of hotels, restaurants and shops.

Mobile Phones
Local SIM cards can be used in European and Australian phones. EU call rates apply for phones using non-Portuguese SIM cards.

Time
Western European Time Zone (GMT/UTC)

Plugs & Adaptors
Plugs have two round pins; electrical current is 220V. British visitors will require an adaptor.

Tipping
Not generally practised.

① Before You Go

Your Daily Budget

Budget less than €50
▶ Dorm beds €15 to €25

▶ Cheap supermarkets and markets for self-caterers

▶ Madeiran buses are an inexpensive way of getting around

Midrange €50–€150
▶ Double room around €90

▶ Two-course dinner with glass of wine €25

▶ Full-day hikes/tours €25 to €35 per person

Top End over €150
▶ Luxury double room from €200

▶ Three-course gourmet dinner from €80

▶ Private transfers and tours

Useful Websites

I Love Madeira (www.ilovemadeira.org) The locals' take on their fascinating island.

Lonely Planet (www.lonelyplanet.com/madeira) Information, bookings and inspiration.

Madeira Rural (www.madeirarural.com) Promotes Madeira's rural tourist industry.

Visit Madeira (www.visitmadeira.pt) Official tourist-board website.

Madeira Web (www.madeira-web.com) Tons of info on culture, tourism and events.

Advance Planning

Six months before If travelling in the peak winter months (November to February), book your flights and hotel well in advance.

One month before Book ferry tickets to Porto Santo and make dinner reservations at the Casino da Madeira.

One week before Arrange your transfer from the airport and book tours and hikes

2 Arriving in Madeira

The overwhelming majority of visitors arrive by air at **Madeira Airport** (www.ana.pt), 12km to the east of Funchal. A small number of travellers now end cruises on Madeira with ships tying up at the cruise terminal within walking distance of Funchal city centre.

From Madeira Airport

Destination	Best Transport
Hotel Zone	SAM Airport bus
Funchal city centre	SAM Airport bus
Machico	SAM bus 113

From Cruise Terminal

Destination	Best Transport
Hotel Zone	Horários do Funchal buses 01, 02 or 04
Funchal city centre	On foot or by taxi
Machico	SAM bus 113

At the Airport

Madeira Airport There are several ATMs, all major and many local car-hire companies are represented and the terminal has a dedicated *Turismo* (tourist office). Put off heavy purchases such as Madeira wine until you reach the airport where you can buy before departure.

3 Getting Around

If you don't hire a car or use taxis, bus is the only way of getting round Madeira. **Horários do Funchal** pushes buses up almost every street in the city (no matter how steep) as well as operating services to selected destinations in the mountainous interior. **Rodoeste** serves the west of the island, **SAM** the east.

Bus

To ride the Horários do Funchal you'll need a magnetic Giro card, which you charge with cash at special terminals. All tickets for other destinations are either bought from the driver, or in the case of Rodoeste from the driver or special booths on Funchal seafront and in Ribeira Brava.

Cable Car

Funchal has two cable-car services – from the Zona Velha to Monte and from Monte to the Jardins Botânicos da Madeira. They both cut journey times considerably but cost much more than the corresponding bus services.

Boat

The boat from Funchal to Porto Santo is the only scheduled ferry service in the archipelago.

Air

The only internal air service in the Madeiran archipelago operates between Madeira and Porto Santo, a quicker, more reliable but considerably more expensive way to go than the ferry.

Madeira Regions

North Coast (p72)
In the rugged north, tall cliffs are pounded by a furious Atlantic and huddling villages boast fascinating tourist attractions.

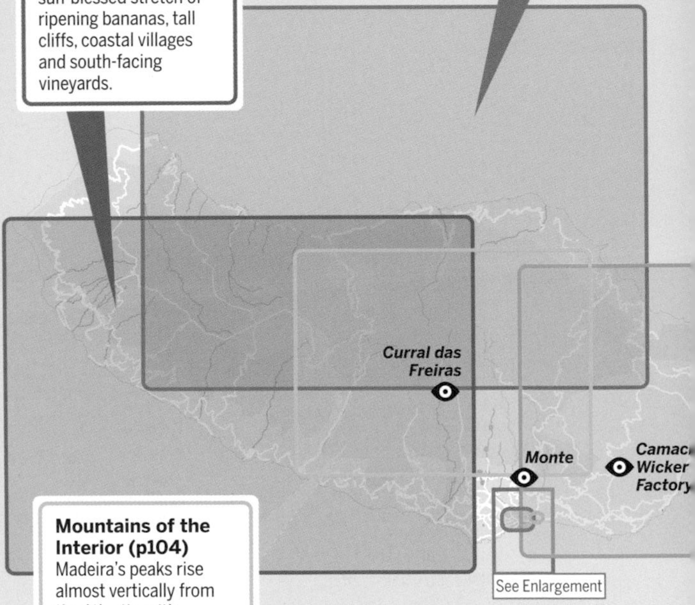

West Madeira (p98)
Madeira's west is a sun-blessed stretch of ripening bananas, tall cliffs, coastal villages and south-facing vineyards.

Curral das Freiras

Monte

Camac Wicker Factory

See Enlargement

Mountains of the Interior (p104)
Madeira's peaks rise almost vertically from the Atlantic, with verdant valleys and the levada channels winding through.

☉ Top Experiences
Curral das Freiras

Worth a Trip
☉ Top Experiences
Monte
Porto Santo

East Madeira (p80)
Planes glide low over the beaches of this densely populated area, and nimble-fingered weavers create wicker wonders.

◉ Top Experiences
Camacha Wicker Factory

Porto Santo ◉

Enlargement

Jardins Botânicos da Madeira ◉

Quinta das Cruzes ◉
Museu de Arte Sacra ◉
Sé ◉

Mercado dos Lavradores ◉
◉ *Zona Velha*

West Funchal (p22)
Some of the island's best museums, a busy city vibe, a vibrant eating scene and Madeira's finest hotels.

◉ Top Experiences
Quinta das Cruzes Museum

Museu de Arte Sacra

Sé

East Funchal (p48)
The eastern half of this energetic city is centred around the atmospheric Zona Velha and the city's main market, both Madeiran must-sees.

◉ Top Experiences
Zona Velha

Mercado dos Lavradores

Jardins Botânicos da Madeira

Explore
Madeira

West Funchal **22**

East Funchal **48**

North Coast **72**

East Madeira **80**

West Madeira **98**

Mountains of the Interior **104**

Worth a Trip

Monte 68

Drive through
Eastern Madeira 78

Levada Paths 88

Porto Santo 112

Racks of drying fish, Câmara de Lobos (p102)
WESTEND61/GETTY IMAGES ©

Explore

West Funchal

The old lanes, wide 20th-century boulevards and pretty squares of the city centre's west are where you'll find some of Madeira's top experiences, its best shopping and most interesting museums. It's also the busiest part of the island with yellow buses, street cafes and shoppers from outside Funchal packing the streets from morning until sundown.

The Region in a Day

☀ Kick off your day in west Funchal with a breakfast of milky coffee and *pastel de nata* (custard tart) at the excellent **A Confeitaria** (p41), from where it's a short walk to one of Funchal's best experiences, the **Quinta das Cruzes Museum** (p24), for a taste of how Madeira's well-heeled once lived.

☀ For lunch head to **Boho Bistrô** (p40) with its imaginative fusion of Madeiran and other cuisines. Take your time as your next stop, the **Museu de Arte Sacra** (p26), doesn't reopen after the lunch break until 2.30pm. After the museum head to Funchal's main church, the **Sé** (p28), once the cathedral for all of Portugal's overseas territories. Almost next door is **Saudade Madeira** (p46), where you can pick up unique souvenirs guaranteed to have been made on the island.

☽ You are really spoilt for choice if you find yourself in the city centre after dark. Stroll along the seafront to see the cruise ships illuminating the harbour wall before retreating to **O Celeiro** (p40) or **Armazém do Sal** (p41) for some hearty Madeiran fare or to **Il Gallo d'Oro** (p40) for something a bit special.

For a local's day in west Funchal, see p30 and p32.

◉ Top Experiences

Quinta das Cruzes Museum (p24)

Museu de Arte Sacra (p26)

Sé (p28)

○ Local Life

Wander along Frente Mar (p30)

Explore São Martinho (p32)

♥ Best of West Funchal

Eating

Boho Bistrô (p40)

O Celeiro (p40)

Il Gallo d'Oro (p40)

Drinking

Cafe do Museu (p43)

Prince Albert Pub (p42)

Shopping

Livraria Esperança (p45)

Saudade Madeira (p46)

Casa do Turista (p45)

Getting There

🚍 **Bus** Almost every bus in Funchal and on Madeira passes through Funchal city centre. From the Hotel Zone take buses 01, 02, 04 and 48.

Top Experiences
Quinta das Cruzes Museum

Now a museum, the Quinta das Cruzes is a quintessential old Madeiran manor house complete with gardens and a private chapel. Originally the home of João Gonçalves Zarco, the Portuguese captain who 'discovered' Madeira, it was remodelled in the 18th century into a stylish home by the wealthy Lomelino family. The exhibits here examine the life of Madeira's well-to-do from the 15th to the 19th centuries in an aptly aristocratic environment – the high-ceilinged mansion is packed with priceless antiques from across the globe.

Map p34, E2

http://mqc.gov-madeira.pt

Calçada do Pico 1

adult/child €3/free

10am-12.30pm & 2-5.30pm Tue-Sun

The garden at Quinta das Cruzes

Don't Miss

Garden

Pleasant to explore before or after a tour of the museum, the garden is a typically exotic example of the type created by the wealthy in the late 19th century. It's a romantically tranquil oasis of mature trees, pebble-patterned pathways, old-fashioned park benches and beds of subtropical plants. Potted orchids grow against the west wall, while on the south side stands a tiny chapel that is normally closed to the public.

Top Floor

The 11 rooms on the building's top floor make up the bulk of the collection. Here, room after room filled with fine furniture, ceramics, tapestry, engravings, oil paintings and jewellery from Europe and beyond give some idea of just how moneyed the merchant classes of Madeira had become by the 18th and 19th centuries. Highlights include the 19th-century oils of Madeira, the glyptic collection, some from Roman times, a typical Madeiran *quinta* (mansion) bedroom and a fascinating section dedicated to Emperor Karl I of Austria, including his priceless Breguet watch.

Lower Floor

Things get a bit chunkier downstairs, with massive wood and hunks of silver replacing the curvaceous Chippendale and delicate fans of the upper floor. Top billing here goes to the Caixa de Açucar, literally 'sugar boxes' (hefty cupboards made from the Brazilian hardwood in which sugar imported to Madeira was packed), a fine example of 16th-century recycling. Other high points include items from Portugal's far-flung Asian colonies, a collection of sedan chairs – once the way to get around the roadless island in comfort – and a huge assemblage of Portuguese silverware.

☑ Top Tips

▶ The garden remains open even when the museum closes for lunch.

▶ There are English-language information sheets in every room.

▶ All bags must be left in lockers at the ticket office.

▶ Hidden behind the ticket office is the 'archaeological park', a collection of old ornate bits of buildings that once graced Funchal's streets.

✗ Take a Break

You'll have to leave the grounds for refreshments. The prettiest cafe around here is the **Teahouse** (Map p34, D1; Calçada do Pico 2-4; ☺8am-5pm Mon-Fri) in the grounds of the Universo de Memórias opposite the museum. Perhaps more apt after a visit to this showcase of how Madeira's rich once lived is the **Prince Charles snack bar** (Map p34, E2; Rua Mouraria 52), a long-established sandwich-and-soup halt opposite the São Pedro Church.

Top Experiences
Museu de Arte Sacra

Madeira's top art collection is housed in the former 16th-century bishop's palace, which dominates one side of Praça do Município. Purchased with the proceeds of Madeira's sugar trade, the highlights of the collection are the priceless pieces of Flemish art commissioned by wealthy Madeiran merchants and landowners for their *quintas* – some of these figures even make a pop-up appearance in the pictures themselves. In the 1950s it was decided to gather all religious art in one place for safe keeping.

👁 Map p34, G2

www.museuartesacra
funchal.org

Rua do Bispo 21

admission €3

🕐 10am-12.30pm & 2.30-6pm Tue-Sat, 10am-1pm Sun

Inside the Museu de Arte Sacra

Don't Miss

Holy Silver

The first rooms you enter contain the museum's dimly lit silver collection, thousands of pieces big and small gleaming magically against dark backgrounds. Solid-silver crucifixes, monstrances, huge plates and teapots come from across the island but mainly from the Sé, giving an indication of the wealth commanded by the world's largest ever diocese (all of Portugal's overseas territories). The highlight is the late-Gothic silver processional cross from the Sé, a truly magnificent piece of 16th-century craftsmanship commissioned by none other than Dom Manuel I.

16th Century to Baroque

The museum's middle section is a procession of 16th- and 17th-century religious oils, handless Gothic statuary and baroque sculpture which once graced Madeira's *quintas* and churches, though a lot of what is on display is from the once very wealthy Convento de Santa Clara. Look out for the almost life-size sculpture of the last supper, a camp-looking Judas holding a bag of cash, and the remarkably well-preserved 17th-century statue of Izabel Rainha de Portugal.

Flemish Masters

Saving the best till last, the undeniable high point of the collection is the four rooms of Flemish masters on the 1st floor. Van Cleve's *Ascension of the Virgin*, *Triptych of the Incarnation* and *Triptych of Saint Peter, Saint Paul and Saint Andrew* dominate one room while Provoost's *Mary Magdalene* from the Church of Madalena do Mar and Morrison's *Nativity* dominate another. Pieter Coeck van Aalst is represented by his impressive *Calvary*, Jesus hoisted high above a lamenting crowd.

☑ Top Tips

▶ No photography or video recordings are permitted in the museum.

▶ The entrance to the museum is on Praça do Município, possibly Funchal's most attractive piazza.

▶ Looking from the museum, to the right you'll see Funchal City Hall, which has an exquisite courtyard lined with *azulejo* tiles and with a tinkling fountain in the middle.

▶ Adjoining the museum is the small, 17th-century Capela de São Luís de Franca, open Tuesday to Friday from 2.30pm to 6pm.

✕ Take a Break

The Cafe do Museu (p43) in the same building is great for a coffee or a meal. **Leque** (Map p34, F2; Praça do Município 7; snacks €1.80-3.20; ◷8am-10pm Mon-Fri, to 6pm Sat, 9am-5pm Sun) is a street cafe serving inexpensive lunch fare and drinks on pretty Praça do Município.

Top Experiences
Sé (Cathedral)

Madeira's principal place of worship sits slap bang in the middle of the city, its tower dominating the skyline as it has since the early 16th century. Though of quite modest proportions, this was once a cathedral that oversaw the largest diocese ever created, one which encompassed all of Portugal's overseas territories. Now it serves just the people of Funchal and Madeira as well as featuring near the top of every tourist's list of essential viewing.

Map p34, G3

www.sefunchal.com

Rua do Aljube

admission free

7am-noon & 4-6.45pm

The cathedral's richly decorated interior

Don't Miss

Interior

Coming in from the bright sunshine outside, it takes a couple of minutes for your eyes to get used to the low-light interior of Madeira's top temple. The first thing you should do is look up – the Sé's intricately carved *alfarje* ceilings are the most elaborate on the island and are made of Madeiran cedar inlaid with shell, rope and white clay to magnificent effect. The other obvious highlight of the interior is the main altar; commissioned by Dom Manuel I, it was crafted between 1512 and 1517. Fully renovated in 2014, its 12 Gothic panels depict the Life of the Virgin and the Passion of Christ.

The Detail

Dom Manuel I went to town on the Sé, showering his favourite church with precious gifts. The baptismal font (on the left as you enter), the pulpit and the processional cross (now on display in the Museu de Arte Sacra, p26) were all gifts from the monarch. Very unusual for Madeira is the memorial brass set in the floor of the north aisle. Confirming Madeira's erstwhile trading links with Flanders, where this sort of brass is common, it depicts wealthy 16th-century merchant Pedro de Brito Oliveira Pestana and his wife.

Exterior

Leaving the dim nave, some parts of the Sé's exterior are worth seeking out. On the south side of the cathedral, look up to find odd barley-twist pinnacles, an architectural feature that belongs to the short-lived Manueline style (1490–1520). The Sé's clock tower has dominated the Funchal skyline for five centuries, though sadly it cannot be climbed.

☑ Top Tips

▶ No tourists may visit the church during the Sunday morning service (11am to noon).

▶ Don't plan your visit for the early afternoon – it's closed!

▶ Photography is permitted throughout the building.

▶ Among the cruise-ship tour groups you will still spot locals praying here, so show respect when exploring.

▶ Best times to visit are just before/after a service when all the lights are on and the carved ceilings are illuminated.

✕ Take a Break

One of Funchal's best cafes, Penha D'Águia (p43), is not far from the Sé's tower, otherwise the cafe at Saudade Madeira (p46) has excellent Madeiran dishes made with local ingredients.

Local Life
Wander along Frente Mar

This sun-drenched walk along the seafront of Funchal's Hotel Zone is the perfect lazy first-day stroll or evening predinner amble. These south-facing slopes are carpeted in tropical and subtropical flora, with lizards darting between rocks and bees busy making exotic honey. The sheer number of cafes, restaurants, beaches and viewpoints along this route provides ample excuse for never reaching the walk's end.

❶ Lido

For years the actual Lido complex has been closed (a new, very 21st-century-looking complex is under construction), but the area still attracts lots of visitors to its restaurants and bars, as well as to the large, palm-fringed grassy area where a football game, tourist kids versus locals, sometimes kicks off.

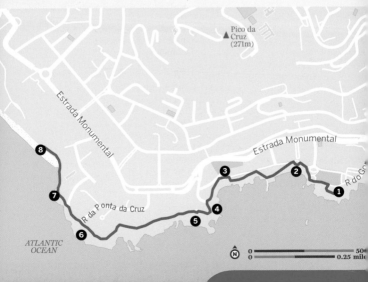

② Ilhéu do Lido

Just past the Lido area you cannot fail to notice the tall tower of rock sticking up just offshore – this is the picturesque Ilhéu do Lido, opposite which is a sunbathing area and stony beach, popular with locals and visiting families. Daring swimmers sometimes brave the Atlantic swell to swim out to the island.

③ Jardim Panorâmico

Up a set of steps from the main route, the terraced **Jardim Panorâmico** (Estrada Monumental; admission free; ⊙7am-10pm) is a sun-catching spot ideal for a lazy afternoon with a book. This is also a superb halt with children as there are go-karts, a bouncy castle and crazy golf, as well as a couple of cafes nearby.

④ Clube Naval do Funchal

A huge sweep of purple bougainvillea announces your arrival at the **Clube Naval do Funchal** (www.clubenavaldofunchal.com; Rua da Quinta Calaça 32; per day nonmembers €10; ⊙9am-6pm), a leisure complex with a restaurant, children's pool, sports facilities, saltwater pool, playground and diving centre.

⑤ Complexo Balnear Ponta Gorda

A more down-to-earth swimming and tanning area is located at Ponta Gorda – the **Complexo Balnear Ponta Gorda** (Ponta Gorda; adult/child €5/free; ⊙9am-6pm). Popular with locals, the pools, cafe-bar, table-tennis area and concrete 'beach' are most popular in summer but stay open all through the winter.

⑥ Ponta da Cruz

A statue of João Gonçalves Zarco looks out towards Cabo Girão from Ponta da Cruz, a huge chunk of rock jutting out into the Atlantic. Bus 2 will take you back from here to the Lido; otherwise enjoy the views then carry on down the steps beyond the statue.

⑦ Doca do Cavacas

Using only locally caught seafood in its dishes, **Doca do Cavacas** (Rua da Ponta da Cruz; mains €11-16.50; ⊙12.30pm-midnight Tue-Sun) juts out of the volcanic rock like an ocean-going liner. The semicircular glazed dining room provides 180-degree Atlantic vistas as you munch on some of its inhabitants.

⑧ Praia Formosa

From the Doca do Cavacas a tunnel bores through the rock to Madeira's biggest beach, Praia Formosa. This starts out as a field of large basalt rocks but beyond the car park becomes a wild stretch of black volcanic sand, the perfect place to chill at the end of your walk.

Local Life
Explore São Martinho

This downhill walk takes you from one of Funchal's best viewing points through the western suburbs to the mid-Atlantic's swishest hotel via lush tropical gardens, slope-hugging villas and some gobsmacking views, most well off the tourist trail. This is where around a quarter of Funchalese live, some in grand residences, others in housing projects, such as Nazaré, making this a diverse stroll.

1 Pico dos Barcelos
Bus 9, 12, 13 or 48 will get you to this *miradouro* (viewing point) 355m above sea level. All of Funchal lies at your feet and when you've finished ogling the panoramic views, there are plenty of cafes to enjoy, as well as a children's playground. It's all downhill from here!

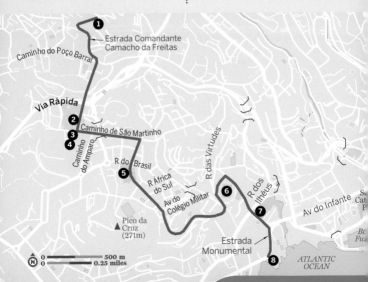

❷ Cemitério de São Martinho

The **Cemitério de São Martinho** (Caminho de São Martinho; ⊙9am-5pm) is well off the tourist path, making it all the more fascinating to visit. Funchal's wealthy were once laid to rest here, their coffins stacked in family *jazigos* – sepulchres resembling small ornate sheds. Art nouveau and functionalist examples are interspersed with neo-Gothic basalt tombs and headstones.

❸ Igreja de São Martinho

High above west Funchal rises the whitewashed spire of the **Igreja de São Martinho** (www.paroquiasmartinho.com; Rua da Igreja; ⊙3-7pm Mon-Fri, 9am-noon & 4-8pm Sat, 9am-1pm Sun), a big, early-20th-century creation. The interior is highly decorative neoclassical in design and the grounds have great views over the west end of the Hotel Zone.

❹ Jardim de São Martinho

Just below the church you'll discover the lovely **Jardim de São Martinho** (Caminha da Igreja Nova; ⊙7am-9pm Apr-Oct, 8am-7pm Nov-Mar), a south-facing, artificially created set of gardens with thousands of exotic plants tumbling down a terraced hillside to a children's playground. Pathways zigzag through the palms, succulents and bursts of blossom as lizards scuttle underfoot.

❺ Mata da Nazaré

This forgotten piece of Funchal greenery sports lots of palm trees and generous stretches of grass, a good spot to shake out the picnic blanket. The only attraction here is the monu-ment to the Combatente Madeirense no Ultramar – Madeirans who died fighting in Portugal's colonies between the 1950s until 1974.

❻ Estádio dos Barreiros

After lapping up the panoramic views from Rua dos Estados Unidos da América you arrive at the newly rebuilt Estádio dos Barreiros, home to Marítimo who play in the highest Portuguese league, the Primeira Liga. Matches normally take place on Sunday afternoons and the atmosphere, whipped up by samba drums and loudhailers, can be pretty good.

❼ Quinta Magnólia

The erstwhile estate of a British merchant family, the Quinta Magnólia Gardens are pleasant enough, though some of the sports facilities could do with an update. The highlight here is the **Biblioteca de Culturas Estrangeiras** (www.bprmadeira.org; Rua Dr Pita, Quinta Magnólia; ⊙9.30am-5pm Mon-Fri), a delightful old relic packed with foreign-language books you can borrow.

❽ Reid's Hotel

The brainchild of Scotsman William Reid, Funchal's first hotel opened its doors in 1891 and is arguably still Madeira's top address. Churchill, Gregory Peck and several crowned heads, among illustrious others, all stayed here and it still attracts a smart set to its formal **tea terrace** (☎291 717 171; www.belmond.com; Estrada Monumental 139; per person €33.50; ⊙3-5.30pm) and sumptuous rooms overlooking Funchal Bay.

For reviews see

◉ Top Experiences p24
◉ Experiences p36
✕ Eating p40
♟ Drinking p42
★ Entertainment p44
🔒 Shopping p45

A B C D

🔒 35

34 🔒

R das Maravilhas

R Calouste Gulbenki

Quinta Cru

9 ◉
Fortaleza
do Pico

Cc do

R Luis de Camões

R do Jasmineiro

17 ✕

Quinta Magnolia

Av do Infante

Quinta Vigia ◉7

Parqu
de San
Catarir

★ 26

20 🔒

Museu CR7

R Imperatriz D'Amélia

◉2

19 🔒

Av Sá Carr

R Carvalho Araujo

Estrada Monumental

27 14
★ ✕

E 11 Jardim de Santa Luzia

F G H

R 5 de Outubro

R Alferes Veiga Pestana

1

R João de Deus

Universo de Memórias João Carlos Abreu
4

Convento de Santa Clara
6

R dos Netos

R 31 de Janeiro

R do Carmo

29

R dos Ferreiros

2

asa Museu Frederico de Freitas
1

Cç de Santa Clara

R de São Pedro

R do Castanheiro

21

31

Museu de Arte Sacra

R Dr Fernão de Ornelas

R do Visconde de Anadia

R Brigadeiro Ouridot

a Carreira

R Mouraria

R das Pretas

R Câmara Pestana

R do Bispo

5

18

R de João Gago

R de Esmeraldo
23

R do Aljube
Sé

R 5 de Outubro

Museu Photographia Vicentes
15

R João Tavira

R da Sé
24

16

R Ivens

Jardim Municipal
8

Av Zarco

R dos Murcas

Praça da Autonomia

13 37

22

R da Alfândega

3

12

R dos Aranhas

Av Arriaga

R Dr António José de Almeida

28

32

36

Av do Mar

3

30

R Conselheiro José Silvestre Ribeiro

Madeira Film Experience

Ventura

25

Marina

Bay of Funchal

4

N 0 0

500 m

0.25 miles

Cruise Terminal

5

Experiences

Casa Museu Frederico de Freitas
MUSEUM

1 ◎ Map p34, E2

Built by the counts of Calçada in the 17th century, this tasteful mansion was purchased by a local lawyer, Frederico de Freitas in the 1940s. An avid collector of just about anything, over the next three decades he proceeded to fill its rooms with antiques and knick-knacks from his travels around the world. (Calçada de Santa Clara 7; admission €3; ☺10am-5.30pm Mon-Sat)

Museu CR7
MUSEUM

2 ◎ Map p34, C5

If after a few days in Funchal, the fact has escaped your attention, now you know: the world's greatest footballer, Cristiano Ronaldo was born and grew up in Funchal. This museum is basically a glitzy public store cupboard for all the tens of cups, man-of-the-match awards, winner's medals, fan letters, hat-trick balls, shirts and golden balls he has acquired throughout his illustrious career. (☎291 639 880; www.museucr7.com; Rua Princesa Dona Amélia 10; admission €5; ☺10am-6pm Mon-Sat)

Madeira Film Experience
CULTURAL EXPERIENCE

3 ◎ Map p34, E3

Funchal's newest attraction ambitiously promises 'the history in 30 minutes' and, it must be said, doesn't disappoint. With a soundtrack in several languages fed to headphones, this superbly produced and animated film takes you through the main periods of the island's past in a dramatic, colourful and informative way, leaving you panting for breath and eager to learn more. (☎291 222 748; www.madeira-filmexperience.com; Marina Shopping, Rua Conselheiro José Silvestre 1, east entrance; admission €5; ☺10.15am-5.45pm)

Universo de Memórias João Carlos Abreu
MUSEUM

4 ◎ Map p34, E2

Housed in an elegant 19th-century mansion, this museum–arts centre is another repository of knick-knacks donated to the city by an avid collector, this time João Carlos Abreu, journalist, writer, politician, actor, artist, former minister of tourism and evidently, keen traveller and souvenir acquirer. However these are no ordinary mementos – room after room is packed with wonderful objects, many works of art. (Calçada do Pico 2; admission €3.50; ☺10am-7pm Wed-Sat)

Museu Photographia Vicentes
MUSEUM

5 ◎ Map p34, F3

Set up by Vicente Gomes da Silva in 1865, this exquisitely preserved photographic studio, above a shady cobbled courtyard, was in use until 1982. The exhibitions of yesteryear's photographic equipment are interesting enough, but the real treasures here are the 800,000

Wax sculpture of Cristiano Ronaldo at Museu CR7

images, mostly from the 20th century, by far the most valuable record of island life in existence. The museum was under renovation at the time of research. (http://photographiamuseuvicentes. gov-madeira.pt; Rua da Carreira 43; admission €3; ⊙10am-12.30pm & 2-5pm Mon-Fri)

Convento de Santa Clara

CONVENT

6 ◎ Map p34, E2

The highlight of this 15th-century convent, once the island's richest, is the beautiful church, one of the island's most attractive, with floor-to-ceiling *azulejo* tiles and waxy hardwood floor. Knock at the adjacent convent door for a short guided tour of the rest

Local Life
Ronaldo's Statue

Wander along the wide, newly revamped walkway between the city centre and the end of the harbour arm and you cannot fail to notice the **Ronaldo statue**, a bronze of Funchal's most illustrious son, Cristiano Ronaldo, unveiled in his presence in December 2014. It depicts the Real Madrid star in his famous 'ready for it' pose, but many have commented on how well endowed the figure is, and they're not talking about his talent with a ball. There was a suggestion the statue could be altered to remove the offending area but the powers that be decided against it.

of the complex given by one of the resident nuns. (Calçada de Santa Clara; admission €2; ⏰10am-noon & 3-5pm)

Quinta Vigia
GARDENS

7 ◉ Map p34, D4

Madeira's president allows visitors into his lusciously old-fashioned gardens packed with time-smoothed pebble walkways, cool fountains and squawking caged birds. Great views of the docked cruise ships. (Avenida do Infante; ⏰irregular hours)

Jardim Municipal
PARK

8 ◉ Map p34, E3

Verdant old park in the city centre, created on the site of the Convent of San Francisco, with tens of exotic labelled trees, twittering birds, basalt pebble paths, a cafe, toilet and a stage where many events are held throughout the year, including part of Carnaval. (Avenida Arriaga)

Fortaleza do Pico
FORTRESS

9 ◉ Map p34, D2

Easy to spot, but taxing to reach, it's worth the slog up to this rocktop fortress northwest of the city centre for the stupendous views. Built in the 17th century as a surveillance point, the building has been Portuguese navy property for the last seven decades (hence the out-of-bounds zones). Undervisited, it's a quiet, if sometimes windy, picnic venue. (Rua do Castelo; admission free; ⏰9am-6pm Mon-Sat)

Parque de Santa Catarina
PARK

10 ◉ Map p34, D4

Large sloping park containing the city centre's best playground, a cafe and Madeira's first chapel. (Avenida do Infante; ⏰7am-9pm Apr-Sep, to 7pm Oct-Mar)

Jardim de Santa Luzia
PARK

11 ◉ Map p34, E1

Created from an old sugar works – hence the huge chimney in the middle and old bits of machinery scattered around the place – this under-visited city-centre oasis has heaps of exotic plantlife, its own levada, a great playground and a cafe. (Rua 31 de Janeiro; ⏰8am-midnight)

DANITA DELIMONT/GETTY IMAGES ©

Jardim Municipal

Understand

Ronaldo

Madeira is football (soccer) mad – you only have to head out in the balmy Atlantic evening to any Funchal park to witness the local kids practising their skills to see for yourself. Funchal, a city of 100,000 somehow manages to keep three teams (Marítimo, União and Nacional) in the top Portuguese league and Portugal's first ever football match took place in the unlikely setting of Camacha. Football, as throughout the Portuguese-speaking world, is a religion as well as a game.

So it arguably comes as no surprise that Funchal has also given the world the best player of the game – *ever,* some claim. Cristiano Ronaldo dos Santos Aveiro (thankfully shortened to Ronaldo) was born in 1985 in the Funchal suburb of Santo António just north of the city centre. It's said his parents, working-class Funchalese, named him after president Reagan. He began his career at Andorinha, a fifth-tier club in Santo António but was soon on his way to Nacional and from there to Sporting Lisbon and Manchester United. In 2009 Ronaldo was sold from there to Spain's Real Madrid for £80 million, making him the most expensive player of all time.

Ronaldo has achieved pretty much all there is to achieve in his sport (though as a Portuguese international he's unlikely to win the World Cup). He has won the Ballon d'Or an amazing three times as well as the UEFA Champions League and the English Premier League. But for all his fame, he certainly hasn't forgotten the island in the Atlantic where it all started – he recently donated many of his trophies, signed shirts and other soccer knick-knacks to enable the creation of the Museu CR7 (p36), now a major Funchal tourist attraction. He's also a regular visitor to Madeira, his mother still lives here, and he can often be seen pulling up his shirt after scoring a goal to reveal an undershirt bearing the single word 'Madeira' daubed in marker pen. The love is mutual, with the football-crazed people of Funchal following their most illustrious son's every move, both off the field and on it.

Eating

O Celeiro
MADEIRAN €€

12 Map p34, E3

One of Funchal's oldest places, 'the barn' tries to live up to its name with rural knick-knackery adorning the walls, but is otherwise a tightly packed, traditionally tiled and beamed Madeiran restaurant serving fish and seafood, as well as a few random dishes, such as pork in curry sauce and lamb chops. (☎291 230 622; www.restauranteoceleiro.com; Rua dos Aranhas 22; mains €7.50-19; ☺noon-3pm & 6-11pm, closed Sun)

Boho Bistrô
BISTRO €€

13 Map p34, E3

Fusion isn't a word used often in Madeiran dining (bananas don't fuse that well), but this funky little urban bistro is attempting something never before tried on the island, and that is to marry traditional Madeiran/

Portuguese flavours with their Asian and South American cousins. Add a contemporary design inserted into a traditional building and the effect is impressive. (☎918 048 432; Rua dos Aranhas 48/50; mains €12-15.50; ☺12.30-3.30pm & 7pm until last customer)

Il Gallo d'Oro
MEDITERRANEAN €€€

14 Map p34, A5

The island's only Michelin star shines brightly from the kitchen of chef Benoît Sinthon, who supplies well-heeled diners with aromatic Mediterranean and gourmet Madeiran fare at the award-winning Cliff Bay Hotel. The renovated interior is surprisingly plain. Smart-casual attire required (jacket for men). (☎291 707 700; www.ilgallodoro.com; Cliff Bay Hotel, Estrada Monumental 147; 3/4/5 courses €70/95/115; ☺8-10.30am & 7-10pm)

Restaurantes dos Combatentes
MADEIRAN €€

15 Map p34, E3

No-nonsense family-run option at one corner of the Jardim Municipal serving scabbard fish, *espetada* (barbecued beef on a skewer), lots of seafood and a couple of tasty vegetarian dishes. The simple dining room is adorned with a few antiques and rural-looking knick-knacks, but otherwise the focus is on honestly prepared local food. (☎291 223 388; cnr Ruas de San Francisco & Ivens; mains €7-16; ☺11.45am-3.30pm & 6-10.30pm)

✅ Top Tip

Bolo de Mel

Invariably described as 'honey cake', the dark-brown wheels of cake known as *bolo de mel* are actually made with molasses (*mel de cana*). Eaten by Madeirans most often at Christmas, but by tourists year round, *bolo de mel* should never be cut, but torn into small chunks. It's often served as an accompaniment to Madeira wine.

Understand
A Trans-Atlantic Pit-Stop

Before air travel, Madeira was a kind of staging post en route to points elsewhere for those travelling by ship across the Atlantic. Captain Cook called in here on one of his voyages of discovery, as did Darwin en route to the Galapagos Islands. Napoleon, however, possibly doesn't quite qualify as a visitor – in August 1815, on the way to exile on St Helena, he was kept aboard the HMS *Northumberland* docked in Funchal Bay – in the warming company of 600 bottles of Madeira wine (a gift from the British consul, it should be added).

But the two most celebrated visitors were piped aboard the good ship Madeira after the two world wars – Austrian Emperor Karl I arrived in exile in 1918, but pneumonia meant he never left. Churchill came to ease his depressive state in 1950 but left quickly after one oil painting and a bottle of Napoleon's wine.

Reid's Palace keeps a special book of illustrious guests, though you really have to be someone to deserve an entry – just 78 have made it onto the list in almost 130 years.

Armazém do Sal
PORTUGUESE €€

16 ✖ Map p34, G3

Housed in an old stone-and-dark-beamed salt store, this is one of the city centre's best restaurants with a different menu to most of its competitors. Wild boar, game and seaweed are more mainland Portugal than Madeira, but scabbard fish and a dessert of pineapple carpaccio brings you right back to the Atlantic's sun-kissed shores. (☏291 241 285; www.armazemdosal.com; Rua da Alfândega 135; mains €13-23; ☺noon-3pm & 6.30-11pm Mon-Fri, 6.30-11pm Sat)

A Confeitaria
BAKERY €

17 ✖ Map p34, C4

This superb busy new bakery with waiter service, opposite the casino, sells cakes and pastries all produced on the premises, plus coffees under €1. Freshness and reasonable prices attract hungry locals to the spartanly funky interior and the pavement tables outside, plus goodies are available for takeaway. (Quinta Victoria, Avenida do Infante; pastries from €0.60; ☺7am-10pm Mon-Fri, from 7.30am Sat & Sun)

Londres
SEAFOOD €€

18 ✖ Map p34, F2

One of the original tourist restaurants around since 1976, the 'London' has a simple no-frills dining room where you can enjoy the classics of Madeiran cuisine plus shellfish, calamari and other nonnative dishes. The service is excellent and another good sign is that it's always packed with locals, especially at lunchtime. (Rua da Carreira 64A; mains €11-15; ⏱11.45am-3.45pm & 6-11.30pm; ✳)

Drinking

Vespas
CLUB

19 🏷 Map p34, C5

Madeira's top nightclub has been around since 1980 and was once the only place on the island for a proper night out. It's still the funnest, funkiest nightspot in these parts and often does its bit for the many festivals that take place in Funchal, such as Carnaval and the Festa da Flor. (Avenida Sá Carneiro 7; ⏱midnight-7am Fri & Sat)

Cafe do Teatro
CAFE

This stylish cafe attached to the Baltazar Dias Theatre (see 28 ⭐ Map p34, E3) is open all day but really comes into its own after dark. Choose from a people-watching spot on the cobbles or head for the courtyard where DJs pump out the latest sounds on a Saturday night. (Avenida Arriaga; ⏱10am-late; 📶)

Prince Albert Pub
PUB

20 🏷 Map p34, C5

Funchal's longest established British pub with sports TV, Sunday roasts, occasional live music and wicker chairs; expat banter adds a strangely colonial atmosphere. (📞291 235 793; Rua Imperatriz Dona Amélia 86; ⏱11am-midnight; 📶)

Copacabana
CLUB

Within the casino (see 26 ⭐ Map p34, D4), some claim this is Funchal's best night out. Music from the '80s and '90s, a resident DJ, regular live acts from Brazil, Madeira and Portugal, screen projection and a sometimes *very* mixed crowd make this one of the liveliest spots in the Atlantic to be when the sun goes down. (www.casinodamadeira.com; Avenida do Infante; ⏱11pm-3am Thu, to 4am Fri & Sat)

Understand
Madeira Wine

Even after you've tasted the island's sweet nectar, you may find yourself asking the question 'just what is Madeira wine?'. Ideally it's made from grapes grown on the island (otherwise it ain't Madeiran). The basic wine is fortified with a type of grappa (usually from mainland Portugal) and left to finish in oak barrels stored in a warm place. The longer the wine is kept, the smoother the taste and the higher the price. As it is a so-called oxidised wine, vintners can even take the wine out of the bottles, clean them and pour the wine back in – the quality is unaffected.

Pedestrians and diners on Avenida Arriaga

Cafe do Museu
CAFE

21 Map p34, G2

Lurking in the loggia of the Museu de Arte Sacra, this is the museum's excellent cafe by day, but after dark it turns into a nightspot, especially at the weekends when it has one of the longest licences on the island. (Praça do Município; ⏰ 9am-midnight Sun-Thu, to 4am Fri & Sat)

Mini Eco Bar
BAR

22 Map p34, F3

Titchy, microspace bar created as ecologically as possible (eco-friendly paints, A-rated electrical appliances), which really comes alive at weekends

when DJs pump out cool tunes for a chilled audience. A great night spot for hanging out with the crowd, though not if you want to sit down. (www.fresh-citrus.com; Rua de Alfândega 3; ⏰ 9pm-midnight Mon & Tue, to 3am Wed-Fri, 10am-2pm & 9pm-3am Sat; 🛜)

Penha D'Águia
CAFE

23 Map p34, G3

Funchal's top chain of bakeries has been milling coffee beans and blackening the surfaces of *pastel de nata* since 1844 and its neatly designed cafes are arguably the best on the island. Cheap, busy and always good quality, they've recently branched out into buffet meals, but it's the unsurpassed coffee and cake most come for. (Rua de João Gago 6-8; ⏰ 7.30am-7pm Mon-Sat, from 8.30am Sun)

Loja de Chá
TEAHOUSE

24 Map p34, G3

Over a hundred teas are available at this tiny tearoom which spills tables out onto sunny Praça do Colombo. Snacks and light lunches accompany the green, black, jasmine and fruit infusions, some on the rather pricey end of the tea scale. (Rua do Sabão 33-35; ⏰9.30am-8pm)

Beerhouse
MICROBREWERY

25 Map p34, E4

The conspicuous assemblage of tent-roofed structures overlook-

ing the marina is Funchal's only microbrewery pumping out a decent German-style lager to go with a typical Madeiran tourist menu. It's spoilt slightly by the burly banana-farmer waiters being trussed up in Bavarian garb, but the beer, cocktails and swish location make it worth a shot. (Pontão São Lazaro; ⏰ 10am-midnight Sun-Thu, to 2am Fri & Sat)

Entertainment

Casino da Madeira
CASINO

26 ⭐ Map p34, D4

Designed by Oscar Niemeyer, the architect behind Brazil's planned capital Brasilia, Madeira's famous casino is a great night out even if you're not a gambler. Follow up the ritzy dinner and show by watching others fritter away their holiday money at the slot machines or with a jig in the Copacabana disco. Smart-casual attire recommended. (www.casinodamadeira. com; Avenida do Infante; ⏰3pm-3am Sun-Thu, 4pm-4am Fri & Sat)

Scat Funchal Jazz Club
JAZZ

27 ⭐ Map p34, A5

This superb little club near the Lido has nightly live music, a wonderful outdoor seating area from which to watch the Atlantic sunset and frequent jam sessions. One of the last

---

Understand
Fado Music

Though it didn't originate on the island, Madeirans share a love of fado music with their mainland cousins and Funchal has at least two places where you can hear it. With roots going back to early 19th-century Portugal, fado is voice and guitar music, often with a mournful, wistful sound and melancholic lyrics describing poverty, loss, longing and life at sea. Its origins are unclear but it has become the signature sound of the Portuguese-speaking world along with the contrasting upbeat samba.

places to close in the Hotel Zone and a commendable dinner menu. (☎291 775 927; www.scatfunchalmusicclub.com; Promenade do Lido; ◷4pm-2am)

Teatro Baltazar Dias

THEATRE

28 ⭐ Map p34, E3

Funchal's grand, late-19th-century main theatre (there were once five!) is the place to head for high-brow entertainment, including classical music, ballet and other performing arts, as well as film festivals and other events. (☎291 215 130; Avenida Manuel de Arriaga)

Shopping

Livraria Esperança

BOOKS

29 🔒 Map p34, F2

This huge shop selling second-hand and new books fills an entire palace and claims to stock over 107,000 titles, making it Portugal's largest. Most of the books are in Portuguese but there is a foreign-language section and it's also a great place to pick up obscure books on Madeiran history, natural history and the like. (www. livraria-esperanca.pt; Rua dos Ferreiros 119 & 156; ◷9am-7pm Mon-Fri)

Casa do Turista

SOUVENIRS

30 🔒 Map p34, E3

Is it a shop, is it a museum? Well, Funchal's most famous souvenir shop

is kinda both. A traditional affair, it's worth taking half an hour to browse the exquisite tableware exhibitions, ceramics, embroidery, wine and tons of other take-home material from Madeira and the Portuguese mainland just to get a comprehensive overview of what the region produces. (Rua Conselheiro José Silvestre Ribeiro 2; ◷9.30am-1pm & 2.30-6.30pm Mon-Fri, 9.30am-1pm Sat)

Fabrica Santo Antonio
FOOD

31 🔒 Map p34, G2

A delightfully old-fashioned shop, with its early 20th-century display cases, scales and counters still in place, from which staff offer the classic made-in-Madeira tooth-rotters such as *bolo de mel* (molasses cake), sugar-cane biscuits and traditional jams. (Travessa do Forno 27-29; ⏰9am-7pm Mon-Fri, to 1pm Sat)

O Bordão
OUTDOOR EQUIPMENT

32 🔒 Map p34, F3

Had to leave your walking sticks at airport security, lost your compass or forgotten your hiking boots for the levadas? Then head for O Bordão (the Staff), the island's only dedi-cated outdoor-gear shop. The range is limited and prices aren't exactly low, but it's just the place to solve a kit emergency. (📞291 281 265; Galerias de São Lourenço, Loja 35, Avenida Arriaga 41-43; ⏰9.30am-7pm Mon-Sat)

Dolce Vita
MALL

33 🔒 Map p34, E3

The Funchal branch of this Portuguese chain of 21st-century malls is the best shopping centre between Lisbon and New York. In addition to the big-name shops, it also has a pharmacy, a large supermarket, cash machines and mobile-phone dealerships. (www.dolcevita.pt; Rua Dr Brito Câmara 9; ⏰9am-10pm)

Fábrica Ribeiro Sêco
FOOD

34 🔒 Map p34, A2

The Fábrica Ribeiro Sêco has revived some of the sugar-processing traditions that once made Madeira wealthy. Buy the island's famous molasses, *bolo de mel*, sugar-cane biscuits and recipe books at the factory, located to the north of the city centre. (www.fabricaribeiroseco.com; Rua das Maravilhas 170; ⏰9am-1pm & 2-6pm Mon-Fri)

Madeira Shopping
MALL

35 🔒 Map p34, A2

Madeira's largest shopping mall situated high above the city centre in the

---

Q Local Life

Saudade Madeira

Local producers of handicrafts and speciality foodstuffs pay for shelf space at **Saudade Madeira** (Map p34, G3; Rua João Gago 2; ⏰ 10am-7pm Mon-Thu, to midnight Fri, to 3pm Sat), an arty shop-cafe in the centre of Funchal. Everything from Madeira-themed paintings to locally made *azulejo* tiles and T-shirts to driftwood art adorn the walls – all unique souvenir material. The cafe sells Madeiran fare and the owners run workshops in the basement. Friday is jazz night.

Displays at Casa do Turista (p45)

Santo António neighbourhood. (www.madeirashopping.pt; Caminho de Santa Quitéria 45; ⏰8.30am-midnight; 🚌8A)

Artecouro
ACCESSORIES

36 🔒 Map p34, F3

This small emporium sells leather goods made from the finest Portuguese hides in Funchal, including belts, handbags, briefcases and wallets. (Rua da Alfândega 15; ⏰10am-1.20pm & 3-7pm Mon-Fri, 10am-1.20pm Sat)

Mercearia Dona Mécia
SOUVENIRS

37 🔒 Map p34, E3

This quaint little shop sells a collection of the best souvenirs and foodstuffs produced on the island, as well as deli produce from Portugal and other countries around the world. (www.donamecia.blogspot.pt; Rua dos Aranhas 30; ⏰10am-7pm Mon-Fri, to 6pm Sat)

Explore

East Funchal

East Funchal is all about the Zona Velha, an old fishers' neighbour-hood that until recently was a rundown and almost lifeless area. Today it's been transformed into a hip quarter packed with bars, galleries, shops and restaurants and is the place to head in Funchal come nightfall. The stellar attraction on the edge of the Zona Velha is the Mercado dos Lavradores, Funchal's vibrant market.

The Region in a Day

☀ Mornings in east Funchal are when the fish market at the **Mercado dos Lavradores** (p52) is in full swing, with fishmongers artfully wielding their sharp gutting knives. When the tuna blood and scabbard fish guts get too much, take a spin around the nearby **Armazém do Mercado** (p64), where local pop-up businesses supply some interesting souvenir ideas.

☀ Buses 30 and 31A leave from near the Casa da Luz for Funchal's unique **botanical gardens** (p54), one of Madeira's definite must-sees. Come back on the same bus or take the cable car to **Monte** (p68), then another cable car back to the Zona Velha.

☾ There's no better place to be in Funchal after dark than the **Zona Velha** (p50), the Atlantic's hottest, funkiest quarter with countless bars and restaurants swamping Rua de Santa Maria until the early hours. The **Venda da Donna Maria** (p61) is the place to head for some authentic Madeiran food; the **Santa Maria Gin Bar** (p62) is a trendy new hang-out for after-dinner drinks, or you could just bar hop all the way back to your hotel.

👁 Top Experiences

Zona Velha (p50)

Mercado dos Lavradores (p52)

Jardins Botânicos da Madeira (p54)

💙 Best of East Funchal

Eating

Gavião Novo (p59)

Oficina (p60)

Hamburgueria do Mercado (p60)

Venda da Donna Maria (p61)

Drinking

Barreirinha Cafe (p62)

Santa Maria Gin Bar (p62)

Shopping

Mercado dos Lavradores (p52)

Madeira Lovers (p66)

Armazém do Mercado (p64)

Patrício & Gouveia (p64)

Bordal (p67)

Getting There

🚌 **Bus** Buses 01, 02 and 04 from the Hotel Zone terminate near the Casa da Luz on the seafront in the Zona Velha. Many other buses from all over Funchal run through the area.

Top Experiences
Zona Velha

Crammed between the Mercado dos Lavradores and the Fortaleza de Santiago, Funchal's 'Old Zone' is the most happening place on Madeira these days. A dilapidated area of abandoned 19th-century fishers' cottages and merchants' houses just a few years ago, this moody neighbourhood of tightly packed streets, basalt arches, tiny chapels and forgotten corners has been transformed into Funchal's nightlife epicentre by the arrival of new and imaginative bars, restaurants and hostels.

⊙ Map p56, C3

Rua de Santa Maria & Rua D Carlos I

Capela do Corpo Santo, Zona Velha

Don't Miss

Rua de Santa Maria

No more than a few metres wide, Funchal's funkiest street runs the entire length of the Zona Velha, its cobbles a car-free throng of tourists and locals from lunchtime to breakfast. By day it's almost blocked in places by the tables and chairs of some of Funchal's best restaurants; by night the crowds spill out of the tiny bars, *ponchas* (alcoholic sugar-cane drink) and caipirinhas in hand. There's also a lot of history in this street, from the diminutive 17th-century **Capela da Boa Viagem**, where it intersects Rua de Boa Viagem, to the tall merchants' houses, their musty cellars harking back to the first settlers and Madeira's days as a place of Atlantic trade. This is also where you'll find the vast majority of artwork belonging to the Open Doors Arts Project (p67).

Largo do Corpo Santo

Rua de Santa Maria widens out towards its eastern end into pretty Largo do Corpo Santo, where there are a couple of low-key attractions amid the tourist-focused restaurants. The **Capela do Corpo Santo** is the old fishers' chapel, though only the 15th-century portal is from the original building. The only section of Funchal's 16th-century city wall to have survived can also be found nearby.

Seafront

Gliding serenely above the red-tiled roofs of the Zona Velha are the cabins of the **teleférico** (cable car; p68), its 21st-century glass-and-steel terminus the dominant feature of the Zone Velha seafront. At the other end is the **Jardim do Almirante Reis**, once a football pitch (hence the footballer statue) but now a place where tourists and Funchalese come to hang out.

☑ **Top Tips**

▶ Try to explore the Zona Velha after dark when all the bars are open.

▶ The cable car from Monte takes you into the Zona Velha.

▶ The Jardim do Almirante Reis is a popular picnicking spot.

✕ **Take a Break**

Madeira Tradicional (p66) is an interesting place to stop for a coffee and a snack, as well as pick up authentic souvenirs. For something more substantial, Venda da Donna Maria (p61) serves bona fide Madeiran fare.

Top Experiences
Mercado dos Lavradores

Bursting with exotic colour, heavy with wonderful mid-Atlantic aromas and busy from morning till late afternoon with a procession of shopping locals and curious tourists, Funchal's main market is one of the city's most captivating attractions. Built in 1940 by architect Edmundo Tavares, this art deco structure has retained the majority of its original features, including very high-quality *azulejos* tiling from the mainland. Far from becoming an ossified tourist attraction, the Mercado still serves as the city's trading hub.

◉ Map p56, B3

Largo dos Lavradores

◷ 8am-7pm Mon-Thu, 7am-8pm Fri, 7am-2pm Sat

Fruit stall, Mercado dos Lavradores

Don't Miss

Flowers

The market's astounding colour begins right at the entrance where local women in folk costume sell all kinds of exotic flowers, shrubs, bulbs and seeds. Over the winter the Madeiran national flower, the bird of paradise *(estrelícia)* is in bloom, a wonderfully striking choice if you're looking for cut flowers. However, throughout the year, a whole array of weird and wonderful triffids is on display, including a selection of the island's famous orchids.

Fruit

For most visitors the fruit stalls around the open central courtyard are the real highlight. For every fruit you recognise there'll be one nearby you don't. Those that grow on Madeira include *anona* (custard apples), *banana ananaz* (monstera), *tomate inglês* (tamarillo) and papaya, as well as, of course, the island's famous sweet miniature bananas. Other fruity treasures include ripe mangoes from Brazil, sweet oranges from the mainland and local grapes; prices are mostly comparable with the island's supermarkets.

Fish

Pass through the fruit market and up the steps for a grandstand view of Funchal's main fish market. The star of the show here are the scary looking *espada* (scabbard fish), black, slippery, eel-like creatures with rows of razor-sharp teeth and huge watery eyes. They are the island's staple fish, caught at night in the depths of the Atlantic. Huge bloodied slabs of tuna also catch the eye, as does the nonchalant skill of the fishmongers as they fillet and hack their way through the day's catch.

☑ Top Tips

▶ Get there early for the fish market – it's as good as over by lunchtime.

▶ Some of the vendors on the upper level are a bit pushy, but normally take no for an answer.

▶ Souvenirs at the market are a bit pricey as it attracts cruise-ship tours with limited time.

▶ To the right of the main entrance is a tiny stall in the shape of an A-frame Santana house selling traditional hand-made Madeiran shoes.

✕ Take a Break

Rooftop **Macaronésia** (⊘same hours as market) is a cafe serving drinks and snacks away from the bustle of the stalls. Otherwise the Mercado dos Lavradores is ringed with cheap cafes and bars – Pau de Canela (p62) is the pick of the bunch.

Top Experiences
Jardins Botânicos da Madeira

Covering 80,000 sq metres, rising from 150m to 300m above sea level and crammed with the most exotic collection of plant life in Europe, Madeira's main botanical garden is like few others. Unlike other institutions of its ilk – normally the preserve of botanists and bored schoolgroups – the Jardins Botânicos da Madeira teem with tourists who wander in amazement at the leafy spectacle on offer. Only created in the 1950s, it's one of Madeira's top tourist attractions.

👁 Map p56, C1

www.sra.pt

Caminho do Meio

admission €5.50

🕘9am-6pm

🚆31/31A

Topiary garden, Jardins Botânicos da Madeira

Don't Miss

Fabulous Flora

There's so much to see here it's difficult to know where to start. Some of the highlights include the Madeiran indigenous and endemic species section, the area of succulents and cacti, the topiary section, the area devoted to medicinal and aromatic plants, the palm tree garden and the formal shrub garden mosaic, one of Madeira's top photo opportunities. Plants to look out for are the *estrelícia* (bird of paradise) that flowers in winter, the mammoth prickly pears with leaves like saw blades, the indigenous *Musschia aurea* with its triffid-like blossoms and the *Geranium maderense* that bursts like a firework in a shower of purple flowers.

Louro Parque

The neighbouring aviary at the southern end can be visited on the same ticket. Here parrots, parakeets, cockatoos, budgies, canaries and warblers squawk and chitter the day away in their spacious cages. The multicoloured birds here are from every corner of the globe but most hail from South America. A colossal, ancient-looking turtle occupies the artificial pond around which some of the cages are arranged.

Hidden Corners

Away from the main areas, the gardens have many hidden corners that are worth seeking out. The Lover's Cave is a fern-lined rocky grotto with a table and chairs made of volcanic pebbles. The *miradouro* (viewing point) has cracking views of the Bom Sucesso creek – controversially, however, the Via Rápida (south coast road) enters a tunnel under the gardens just below this spot, which spoils the effect somewhat. In another nook you'll discover a typical Santana A-frame house.

☑ Top Tips

▶ All plants are labelled with scientific name, common name, family and country of origin.

▶ Feeding the birds in the Louro Parque is not permitted.

▶ Maps are located at strategic spots and explanations are in English.

▶ Take bus 31/31A or the **cable car** (www.teleferico jardimbotanico.com, single/ return €8.25/12.75) from Monte.

✗ Take a Break

The only place to take a break at the gardens is the **snack bar** (Jardins Botânicos da Madeira; snacks €2-4; ⊙9am-5pm) on the northwest side. It's pricey by Madeira's standards but a sun trap with stupendous views.

For reviews see

◉ Top Experiences	p50
◎ Experiences	p57
✕ Eating	p59
⊗ Drinking	p62
◉ Entertainment	p64
⊕ Shopping	p64

Swimmers at a sea platform near Barreirinha Cafe (p62)

Experiences

Casa da Luz –
Museu de Electricidade   MUSEUM

1 ◉ Map p56, A4

Decommissioned in 1989, Funchal's old power station, still the headquarters of EEM (Empresa de Electricidade da Madeira – Madeira Electric Company), has been turned into a museum dedicated to the history of electricity generation on the island and to electricity itself. Downstairs a huge hall holds the old diesel generators but the fun really starts upstairs where you'll find many interactive, electricity-related exhibits.

(www.museucasadaluz.com; Rua Casa da Luz 2; adult/child €2.70/free; ☺10am-12.30pm & 2-6pm Tue-Sat)

Jardins do
Palheiro   GARDENS

2 ◉ Map p56, E1

Some 500m up in the hills east of Funchal, these much-loved subtropical gardens are a beautiful mix of formal and 'wild' areas with thousands of unusual and familiar plants. After a good walk, retreat to the tearoom to refuel. (www.palheirogardens.com; Caminho da Quinta do Palheiro 32; adult/child €10.50/free; ☺9am-5.30pm)

IBTAM   MUSEUM

3 ◉ Map p56, B2

IBTAM is the organisation that oversees Madeiran embroidery production – anything bearing its label is guaranteed to be the genuine, locally made article. This quaint museum at IBTAM's headquarters examines many aspects of traditional embroidery with mock-ups of 19th-century rooms awash with embroidered textiles. A film at the end of the exhibition looks at the island's traditional industries and IBTAM's role. (Rua Visconde de Anadia 44; admission €2.50; ☺ 9.30am-12.30pm & 2-5.30pm Mon-Fri)

Museu do Brinquedo   MUSEUM

4 ◉ Map p56, B3

This toy museum occupies seven rooms at the Armazém do Mercado and is essentially made up of the 20,000-piece private collection of one José Manuel Borges Pereira. More for dads than kids, it's an I-used-to-have-one-of-those-in-the-'70s sort of experience with everything from Corgi and Dinky cars to Action Man and Star Wars figures on display. (2nd fl, Armazém do Mercado, Rua Hospital Velho 28; adult/child €5/3; ☺10am-6pm)

Fortaleza de Santiago   FORTRESS

5 ◉ Map p56, D4

The ochre and dark-pink fortress that caps the Zona Velha seafront was built in the first half of the 17th century when Funchal was vulnerable to pirate attack. The art museum inside isn't much to shout about but the fun here is scrambling around the various rooms, turrets, battlements and hidden corners, some providing great photo ops. (Rua de Santa Maria; museum €2, fortress free; ☺museum 10am-12.30pm & 2-5.30pm Mon-Sat, fortress 10am-11pm)

Fortaleza de Santiago

Igreja do Socorro CHURCH

6 ⊙ Map p56, E4

This impressive clifftop church at the eastern end of the Zona Velha is a 1750 rebuild – the original was destroyed in the earthquake of 1748. Slightly off the tourist trail and looking out across the Atlantic in all its baroque pomp, it boasts some impressive *azulejos* tiling and a painted ceiling atmospherically dulled by the smoke of a million candles. (Largo do Socorro; ⊙8.30am-6pm)

Quinta da Boa Vista GARDENS

7 ⊙ Map p56, E1

Founded by former Honorary British Consul Cecil Garton, this garden is the best place to experience Madeira's exquisite orchids. The orchid houses are a riot of *Cattleyas*, *Cymbidiums* and *Paphiopedilums* but the rest of the place could do with a tidy round. (Rua Lombo da Boa Vista; adult/child €4.50/ free; ⊙9am-5.30pm Mon-Sat)

Eating

Gavião Novo SEAFOOD €€

8 ⊗ Map p56, C3

Madeira's top seafood restaurant is an intimate affair at the heart of the Zona Velha, attracting tourists, locals and Portuguese rich and famous, who come for the most authentic dining experience on the island. Only fish

English Menus

We have yet to find an eatery on Madeira that didn't have an English menu, or one in German, French and Spanish for that matter, though translations can be a bit ropey and sometimes amusing. Very few waitstaff have problems communicating in English, even in the remotest of places.

from the waters around Madeira are used and other ingredients come from the owner's estate in the island's north. (www.gaviaonovo.pt; Rua Santa Maria 131; mains €8-16; ⊙noon-11pm)

Hamburgueria do Mercado
BURGERS €

9 🍴 Map p56, B3

Humungous gourmet burgers are the dining attraction at this joint within the Armazém do Mercado complex. The interior is all chunky wood and naked concrete, the Mercado burger a huge slab of beef oozing with five different cheeses, the beer local (Corral) and the bill small. Filling, cheap, honest and with a cool soundtrack, too. (Armazém do Mercado, Rua Latino Coelho 41; burgers €3-8.50; ⊙noon-midnight)

Oficina
INTERNATIONAL €

10 🍴 Map p56, B2

Minimalist, hip and innovative, this new bar-cafe at the entrance to the Armazém do Mercado is one of the few places between Lisbon and Bermuda where you'll successfully track down a veggie burger. Hotdogs, soups, homemade cakes (actually made in someone's home) and rare Belgian beer inhabit the menu, events such as DJ nights and local live music the calendar. (Armazém do Mercado, Rua Hospital Velho 28; mains €3-5; ⊙9.30am-8pm Mon-Thu & Sat, to midnight Fri, to 6pm Sun)

Santa Maria
INTERNATIONAL €€

11 🍴 Map p56, C3

This snazzy, minimalist restaurant belonging to Funchal's top hostel serves up lobster, fish burgers, local limpets and sushi on square plates. The bar is made of sardine cans, the lightbulbs are bare, the staff efficient and the courtyard out back an oasis of peace when the party gets going on Rua de Santa Maria. (www.santamariafunchal.com; Rua de Santa Maria 145; mains €8-18.50; ⊙11am-midnight)

Riso
INTERNATIONAL €€

12 🍴 Map p56, E4

The menu at this restaurant abutting the Fortaleza de Santiago is a rice-themed trip around the world, every dish (even the desserts) containing basmati, Thai, arborio, wild or venere. The terrace has unobstructed Atlantic vistas, meaning you may linger longer over your risotto than you originally intended. (www.riso-fx.com; Rua de Santa Maria; mains €13-21; ⊙12.30-2.30pm & 7-10.30pm Tue-Sun)

Local street scene

Tasca Literária MADEIRAN €€

13 Map p56, B3

The theme here is a little obscure but with a blood-red and basalt interior and black-and-white photos of famous Madeirans on the walls, it's an atmospheric place to spend an evening in the Zona Velha. Plates come laden with portions of *espada* (scabbard fish), tuna, rabbit, goat and lamb and the wine flows freely. Reservations advised Friday and Saturday evenings. (☎291 220 348; Rua de Santa Maria; mains €11-21; ☺10am-midnight)

Local Life
Venda da Donna Maria

One of the best places to sample real Madeiran food is **Venda da Donna Maria** (Map p56, B3; ☎291 621 225; Rua de Santa Maria 51; mains €12-20; ☺11am-11pm, to midnight Fri & Sat), a great shabby-chic Zona Velha restaurant that uses local recipes every Funchal *avozinha* (granny) would recognise. Take a seat at the tightly packed jumble of tables to enjoy *espada* (scabbard fish) with banana, São Martinho codfish and lots of other genuine Madeiran favourites.

Drinking

Barreirinha Cafe
BAR

14 🚇 Map p56, E4

Outside-only cafe-bar above the *complexo balnear* (swimming complex) at the eastern end of the Zona Velha offering snacks and drinks to the sound of brine on basalt any time of day. Weekend DJs and a real mixed crowd. (Largo do Socorro 1; 🕙 8am-midnight Sun-Thu, 8am-2am Fri & Sat)

Santa Maria Gin Bar
BAR

15 🚇 Map p56, C3

A welcome addition to the Zona Velha drinking scene, this cool hostel gin bar has 35 types of mother's ruin, which you can enjoy as you melt into an armchair to the gentle sounds of

---

Understand
Coffee

Forget espressos and lattes, the bean-crazed Portuguese have their own words for their brews. A *bica* is a shot of coffee – an espresso; a *garoto* is 50% espresso, 50% milk. A *chinesa* is a strong milky coffee, while a *carioca* is a weak espresso. A *galão* is as close to a latte as you're going to get and is served in a glass. Alternatively you could just have a good ole cuppa *chá* (tea).

---

piped jazz, a few plates of tapas at your elbow. Regulars store their bottle of gin in a special locker and keep the key for next time. (Rua de Santa Maria 149-151; 🕙 6pm-late)

Pau de Canela
CAFE

16 🚇 Map p56, B3

Old-school bakery-cafe next to the Mercado, usually inhabited by working-class Funchalese families, market workers and the odd pigeon, all of whom come to feed on cheap pastries, cakes, pizzas, made-in-front-of-you sandwiches and toasties. Don't lose your chit, as you pay at the door as you leave. The most expensive item on the menu costs €2. (Rua Latino Coelho 10; snacks €0.50-2; 🕙 7am-8pm Mon-Fri, to 1pm Sat)

Mercearia da Poncha
BAR

17 🚇 Map p56, C3

Specialising in Madeiran *poncha* (alcoholic drink made with sugar-cane spirit, sugar, lemon and water), this small Zona Velha bar often crams Rua de Santa Maria with drinkers until the early hours. A lively atmosphere is always guaranteed. (Rua de Santa Maria 154; 🕙 5pm-2am Tue-Sun)

Venda Velha
BAR

18 🚇 Map p56, C3

This bar-restaurant attempts to recreate the shop-tavern of the early 20th century, once the community

Understand
Potted History
– –

Recent studies have shown that Madeira is a mere seven million years old, formed by volcanic activity which thrust a mass of rock and lava through the Atlantic's choppy waters. Never inhabited by 'natives', the island spent millennium after tranquil millennium unacquainted with the human race.

So just who got to Madeira first? The Portuguese history books would have us believe it was captain João Gonçalves Zarco, dispatched in 1419 and 1420 by Prince Henry the Navigator who was acting on a hunch. However, a Medici map of 1351 shows the Madeiran Archipelago and even the Romans may have been aware of it – Pliny the Elder mentions the islands in his *Natural History*.

But it was Zarco et al who really kicked off the human story on Madeira and Porto Santo. He became governor of half the island (fellow explorer Tristão Vaz Teixeira got the other half) and established Funchal, which quickly took over from Machico as the island's capital.

As more and more settlers from Europe arrived, at first the area around Funchal was used for wheat production, but sugar cane was soon found to be a more lucrative prospect. Madeira's year-round warmth meant grapes began to thrive and Madeira wine became a vital export. This was helped by the British occupation of Madeira during the Napoleonic wars – Madeira wine became a luxury tipple in Victorian Britain and British merchants were given special trading rights with the island.

The first wealthy tourists also arrived on the coast in the late 19th and early 20th century, but this was in stark contrast to conditions inland where hunger stalked the land.

The two world wars left Madeira almost untouched. In 1974 the Carnation Revolution in mainland Portugal led to Madeira being handed autonomous status with its own legislative assembly and president. With the building of the airport in the 1960s tourism became the mainstay of the economy and that remains the case to this day. In the new millennium some big infrastructure projects such as the south coast motorway (the Via Rápida) have improved life on Madeira immensely. No doubt Zarco would have approved.

hubs across the island. Special focus here falls on Madeiran *poncha,* a more alcoholic drink than many non-Madeirans imagine – head here after midnight to see what we mean. (www.vendavelha.com; Rua de Santa Maria 170; ⊘noon-4am)

23 Vintage Bar   CLUB

19 🎧 Map p56, B3

Celebrating the music of the 1960s to 1990s, this great little club-bar livens up weekends in the Zona Velha. Friday night is all about paying nostalgic tribute to an iconic band or artist such as Modern Talking, Kylie Minogue, Lenny Kravitz or U2; more eclectic Saturday is normally Jukebox night. (Rua de Santa Maria 27; ⊘8pm-2am Fri & Sat)

Local Life
Armazém do Mercado

Exquisitely renovated by architect Paulo David, the man behind Calheta's Casa das Mudas, the **Armazém do Mercado** (Map p56, B3; www.armazemdomercado.com; Rua Hospital Velho 28 & Rua Latino Coelho 39; ⊘10am-8pm Mon-Sat, to 6pm Sun) is an old embroidery factory that has been transformed into an urban pop-up space for local businesses and artisans, as well as housing the Museu do Brinquedo (p58) and a couple of hip eateries. There's an organic produce market every Saturday morning.

Entertainment

Arsenio's   LIVE MUSIC

20 ⭐ Map p56, C3

The aroma of a loaded charcoal grill wafts along Rua de Santa Maria from Arsenio's, luring evening strollers into the old, atmospheric dining room, all basalt floors, ancient beams and leather chairs. Every evening from 7pm to 11pm, meals are taken with a dose of fado, Arsenio's being the best place on Madeira to experience Portugal's signature musical genre. Book ahead for the best seats. (📞291 224 007; Rua de Santa Maria 169; ⊘noon-late)

Sabor e Fado   LIVE MUSIC

21 ⭐ Map p56, C3

Though not as illustrious as other Funchal fado-and-dinner venues, Sabor e Fado is nonetheless an intimate affair. The menu is meat heavy; the live music starts at 7pm and the staff often gets in on the act. (Travessa das Torres 10; ⊘6pm-1am Thu-Tue)

Shopping

Patrício & Gouveia   SOUVENIRS

22 🔒 Map p56, B2

Funchal's classiest souvenir emporium is a world away from the bird-of-paradise-flower fridge magnets and chinese T-shirts of the Hotel Zone. This venerable institution brings together the finest handicrafts and foodstuffs Madeira has to offer, with the

Understand
Madeira's Traditional Culture

One of the many pleasures to be sampled on Madeira is the island's traditional culture, always a vividly colourful experience at any time of year. In addition to the list of festivals that pack out every week of the calendar, there's a lot to see year-round across the island, from embroidery demonstrations to food fairs and folk dancing in the streets of Funchal to tasting sessions in ancient wineries.

Folk dancing has become much more accessible in recent years as more hotels and restaurants host performances. Dancers normally don the Madeiran folk costume for the occasion (baggy trousers, white shirt and odd goat-skin shepherd's boots for the men; traditional striped cloth dress and white blouse for women). Both sexes pop a comical *carapuca* on their heads – a black pointed skullcap. Songs are warbled to the accompaniment of the *rajão* or *braguinha* (a kind of mandolin), a drum, castanets and a *raspadeiro* (a notched stick played like a washboard). You may also see the ensemble bashing the ground with a *brinquinho* – a jangling stick of puppets and small bells.

Music and dance are also essential elements in the many food festivals that happen across Madeira. Festivals including Curral das Freiras (chestnuts), Faial (custard apples), Jardim da Serra (cherries), Madalena do Mar (bananas), Câmara de Lobos (scabbard fish), Funchal (wine), Porto da Cruz (grapes), Ponta do Pargo (apples), Santo da Serra (cider), Ponta do Sol (sugar cane), Santana (lemons) and Caniço (onions) celebrate the best of all that grows in Madeira's volcanic soils or is hooked out of the bountiful Atlantic.

Wicker production and embroidery are the two main traditional handicrafts, but there are of course other, smaller-scale industries. Cottage jewellery production has taken off in recent years and items are available from stalls in the Armazém do Mercado and from Saudade Madeira (p46). Scrimshaw involves carving intricate figures from whale bone – this can be found at small stalls on the seafront in Caniçal, but don't worry – all the bone used comes from Madeira's now defunct whaling industry. Traditional tile production has also come to Madeira, many of the designs exotically Moorish affairs.

Colourful door art in the Zona Velha

company's own embroidery the star of the show. (☎291 222 723; www.patricio gouveia.pt; Rua Visconde de Anadia 34; ⊗9am-1pm & 3-6.30pm Mon-Fri, 9.30am-noon Sat)

Madeira Tradicional   FOOD & DRINK

23 🔒 Map p56, C3

Great little shop-cafe-bar selling exclusively Madeiran/Portuguese wares such as olive oil, soap, *poncha*, *bolo de mel*, sugar-cane biscuits, trendy souvenirs, Madeiran table wines, locally made jewellery and much more. On Fridays and Saturdays, the tiny cafe turns into a late-night Zona Velha drinking spot. (www.madeiratradicional.pt; Rua de Santa Maria 141; ⊗ 10.30am-7pm Mon-Thu, to 2am Fri & Sat)

Madeira Lovers   SOUVENIRS

24 🔒 Map p56, B3

The antidote to Madeira's often fusty souvenirs, this cool new company has come up with contemporary designs for its mementos, providing a fresh, 21st-century alternative to plastic dolphins and toboggan driver's hats. Trendy T-shirts, Madeira-themed notebooks and grafitti postcards, as well as local jewellery and CDs of local music, are just some of the things it offers. (www.madeiralovers.com; Armazém do Mercado, Rua Hospital Velho 28; ⊗10am-7pm, to 6pm Sun)

Understand
Door Art of the Zona Velha

Strolling through the Zona Velha you cannot fail to notice the area's weird and wonderful door art, created as part of the **Projecto Arte Portas Abertas** (Open Doors Arts Project; www.arteportasabertas.com). The idea to spice up the rather derelict doors and gates of the area is the brainchild of Spanish artist José Maria Zyberchema, who since 2011 has been inspiring local artists and arty locals to splash works of public art across the Zona Velha. The project has been credited with giving a huge lift to what was becoming a very run-down chunk of Funchal – a now quickly revitalising Zona Velha has become the nightlife hub of the Madeiran capital. The artist hopes the idea might spread to other communities across the island – some similar art can already be seen on the old doors of Machico.

Bordal

HANDICRAFTS

25 🔒 Map p56, A2

Bordal is Madeira's top embroidery company, its mark (a hologram) a guarantee the item you are buying has been made on the island. The shop specialises in fine embroidered linens and the factory upstairs can also be visited free of charge. Women come here daily to pick up and drop off work which they complete at home. (www.bordal.pt; Rua Dr Fernão Ornelas 77; ⊘shop 9am-1pm & 2-7pm Mon-Fri, 9am-1pm Sat, factory to 6pm Mon-Fri only)

Fabrica de Chapeus de Santa Maria

ACCESSORIES

26 🔒 Map p56, D4

Tiny, old, ramshackle Zona Velha workshop where traditional Madeiran hats are sewn together amid piles of headgear, ancient sewing machines and scraps of material. Hours are erratic. (Rua de Santa Maria 238-9; ⊘11am-7pm Mon-Fri)

Top Experiences
Monte

Getting There

🚡 The **Teleférico do Funchal** (single/return €10/15; 🕙9am-5.45pm) runs from the seafront.

🚌 Bus 21 terminates at Largo da Fonte, bus 22 at Babosas. Bus 48 links Monte directly with the Hotel Zone.

Roosting high above Funchal, this aristocratic villa quarter was once the stomping ground of wealthy families who preferred summer's lower temperatures 500m up. Today it's one of Madeira's must-sees, with a cluster of sights interspersed with outlandish greenery and infused with refreshingly cool and exotically perfumed air. Getting here is also part of the fun with the cable car from the Zona Velha often taking visitors above the low clouds that wreathe Madeira's mountain sides.

Traditional toboggan ride

Don't Miss

Igreja da Nossa Senhora

Some 68 stone steps climb dramatically to the doors of one of Madeira's finest churches, Monte's Igreja da Nossa Senhora. Rising in eye-balancing baroque symmetry, it was built in the wake of the 1748 earthquake which destroyed the original. The huge baroque altar bears the tiny statue of Our Lady, one of the most revered icons on the island. However a side chapel to the left as you enter attracts most attention – this contains the tomb of exiled Austrian Emperor Karl I (see box, p71).

Toboggans in the Sun

Ernest Hemingway described it as the 'most exhilarating experience' of his life – whether he was attempting a little sarcasm, we'll never know, but nonetheless the toboggan ride down to Livramento is a must-have experience. Toboggans were once the only way goods could be carried across Madeira's steep and roadless landscapes and the Monte *carros de cesto* are a relic of those days. The toboggans are made of Camacha wicker with padded seats for two people. The drivers wear straw boater hats, white shirts, white trousers and shoes with rubber soles which help them brake the toboggan's plunge down the asphalt. Ten minutes of slithering for €30 (two people) may seem as steep as the slope you are descending, but it's a unique experience, though possibly not as exhilarating as Papa described it.

Remnants of a Railway

The only train to ever run on Madeira was a rack-and-pinion service that climbed 4km from the city centre to Monte and then on to Terreiro da Luta between 1893 and 1943. The one-carriage train was a major tourist attraction (as the cable

---

Monte is 3km as the crow flies from the Funchal seafront.

www.telefericodo
funchal.com

☑ Top Tips

▶ Weather in Monte can differ enormously to the conditions down in Funchal. If you can't see the Igreja da Nossa Senhora from the coast, it's likely to be damp and cold up there.

▶ Services at the Igreja da Nossa Senhora take place Tuesday, Wednesday, Friday and Saturday at 6pm, Thursday at 8.30am and Sunday at 8am and 11am.

✕ Take a Break

Cafe do Parque (Largo da Fonte; mains & snacks €1-9; ⏱9am-5pm) on Monte's atmospheric old square is a pretty spot for coffee and cakes.

Alto Monte (Caminho das Tihas; mains €6-18; ⏱11am-3pm & 8-11pm) is a recently spruced-up cafe playing it safe with Madeiran favourites.

Teleférico (cable car) to Monte

next to the road. Plans to revive the Monte–Terreiro da Luta section of the line are on hold.

Monte Palace Tropical Gardens

One of the highlights of any visit to Monte is a wander round the **Monte Palace Tropical Gardens** (www.monte palace.com; Largo da Fonte, Monte; admission €10; ⊙9.30am-6pm). This former hotel began life in the late 18th century as a private residence belonging to the British Consul Charles Murray. In the late 1980s it was purchased by local entrepreneur José Berardo who transformed it into a weird-and-wonderful tourist attraction by filling the grounds with fountains, grottoes, follies, sculpture pieces and lots of exotic plant life.

Teleféricos

The most interesting way to reach Monte is on the cable car from the Zona Velha, a major engineering project completed in 2000. The 20-minute ride above the red rooftops, banana trees and plunging gorges of Funchal is an unforgettable experience but definitely not one for vertigo sufferers. The swaying cabins deliver visitors to Barbosas, a short walk from Monte's sights. Nearby another less-frequented cable car heads across to the botanical gardens.

car is today) hauling wealthy tourists up from the city centre. However a couple of accidents and bankruptcy put paid to the service – all that's left of those days is the almost completely straight Via do Comboio (Train St) that follows the route of the tracks, a railway viaduct in Monte just off Largo da Fonte and Monte's old railway station which stands in a forlorn state on the corner of the square

Understand
The Last Habsburg

There's an unexpected historical full stop on the island of Madeira, a place that witnessed the last act of a centuries-old story, far away from its main central European stage. As every Austrian royalist knows, Monte is the final resting place of the last Habsburg, exiled Emperor of Austria and last king of Bohemia and Hungary – Karl I.

But how did the final line in the story of the Habsburgs, a dynasty that dominated European royal history for eight centuries, come to be written on an island in the Atlantic? Following the assassination of Austrian Archduke Franz Ferdinand in Sarajevo in 1914, the event that lit the blue touch paper of WWI, Karl became heir presumptive and when Emperor Franz Joseph died in November 1916, he succeeded to the Austrian throne. But by 1918 the Austrian empire was in tatters, new countries such as Czechoslovakia and Hungary being forged out of the ruins. With an Austrian Republic declared in 1919, Karl refused to abdicate or give up his claim to sovereignty and fled to Switzerland in March of that year.

After a couple of unsuccessful stabs at reclaiming the Hungarian throne, in November 1921 the British decided to exile Karl I and his wife to Madeira, a place from which it was thought he couldn't easily make another attempt. Originally billeted in the Villa Victoria near Reid's Palace Hotel, the family were later moved up to Monte and the Quinta do Monte. On a stroll into town, the unlucky Habsburg caught a cold which developed into pneumonia. He died on 1 April, 1922.

Beatified by Pope John Paul II in 2004, Karl's body lies in a simple flag-draped casket in a side chapel in Monte's Igreja da Nossa Senhora. Over the decades there has been talk of transferring the body to the Imperial Crypt in Vienna but nothing has ever come of this. The chapel has become a shrine for royalists from across the former Habsburg empire who come to seek out this place where the Habsburg story came to its unlikely but definitive end.

Explore

North Coast

Madeira's rugged north coast often feels a world away from the sun-splashed south, with high cliffs rising vertically from the seething Atlantic that pounds the island with full force. Three villages have sufficient attractions for a day excursion from Funchal; but remember – while the south coast bathes in sunshine, the chilly north's damp air might mean it's time to fish the sweaters out.

The Region in a Day

☀ With a car all the sights along the north coast can be covered in a long day (it's simply not possible by bus). Head along the Via Rápida and then follow the signposts from Machico to Santana, a village famous for its **A-frame houses** (p76; pictured left). The tourist office occupies one of them. With kiddies along for the ride, the **Parque Temático da Madeira** (p75) is the place to let off steam and learn lots about the island in the process.

☀ A short drive along the coast, there's more educational activity at the **Grutas e Centro do Vulcanismo** (p75) in São Vicentes. There are a few cafes in the village where you can have lunch before or after you delve deep into the earth's core to see how Madeira was formed. The local beach is a good place to collect pumice.

☾ Evening is a special time to arrive in Porto Moniz, mainly as you'll have the place entirely to yourself. Watch the sun set and ponder the vastness of the Atlantic, perhaps with a drink at **Cachelote** (p77) with views across the volcanic rock pools, before heading back to Funchal and dinner.

♥ Best of the North Coast

Villages
São Vicente (p133)

For Kids
Aquário da Madeira (p75)

Centro Ciência Viva (p75)

Grutas e Centro do Vulcanismo (p75)

Parque Temático da Madeira (p75)

Eating
Cantinho da Serra (p76)

Getting There

🚗 **Car** The best way to travel the sights of the north coast is with your own set of wheels.

🚌 **Bus** The following buses serve the north coast from Funchal: Porto Moniz, Rodoeste bus 80, 139; São Vicente, Rodoeste bus 139; Santana, Horários do Funchal bus 56.

ATLANTIC OCEAN

For reviews see
Experiences p75
Eating p76

⊙ Experiences
✕ Eating

10 km
5 miles

Porto Moniz 2
Aquário da Madeira 2
Centro Ciência Viva 10
3

Ribeira da Janela

ER101
VE2
Seixal

11
12 ✕ **São Vicente**
Grutas e Centro 1
do Vulcanismo

ER104

Ponta Delgada ⊙ 5
Igreja do
Bom Jesus

ER101

Santana
7 ✕ 9
✕ ✕ 4 8

*Parque Temático
da Madeira*

Faial

Porta da Cruz 6

Ribeiro

Quemadas
Forest Park

Pico das Torres
(1853m)
Pico do
Arieiro

Pico Ruivo
(1862m)

Encumeada
Pass

ER110

Experiences

Grutas e Centro do Vulcanismo

CAVE

1 🎯 Map p74, B3

Top billing on Madeira's north coast goes to this two-for-one attraction just south of São Vicente. The first part of the experience is a guided tour of local caves – 900,000-year-old lava tubes studied by English geologist James Johnson in the 1850s. The second is the Centro do Vulcanismo, a 3D, interactive look at Madeira's volcanic birth and volcanoes in general. (www.grutasecentro dovulcanismo.com; Sitio do pé do Passo, São Vicente; adult/child €8/6; ☺10am-7pm)

Aquário da Madeira

AQUARIUM

2 🎯 Map p74, A2

Madeira's top aquarium hides away like a hermit crab in a renovated stone fortress. Inside, 12 tanks represent various ocean habitats around Madeira, the biggest of these containing 500,000L of water and big enough to accommodate divers. (Rua Forte São João Batista, Porto Moniz; adult/child €7/4; ☺10am-6pm)

Centro Ciência Viva

MUSEUM

3 🎯 Map p74, A2

The Madeira branch of a national museum, which covers a wide range of scientific topics in an imaginative, hands-on way. Here the focus is on Madeira's Unesco-listed laurisilva forests, their climate, biodiversity and the human relationship with it.

Porta da Cruz (p76)

Interactive exhibits include a bare-foot forest-floor walk, a virtual levada and heaps of other touchscreens, puzzles and films. (www.portomoniz.cienciaviva.pt; Rotunda do Ilhéu Mole, Porto Moniz; adult/child €3.50/2.50; ☺10am-6pm)

Parque Temático da Madeira

AMUSEMENT PARK

4 🎯 Map p74, E3

An engaging place to take the kids, this Madeira-themed park has a boating lake, a maze, a Monte train, mock-ups of Santana A-frame houses, a large kiddies' playground, Madeira-specific exhibitions and a cafe. It's quite informative but not worth a special trip from

Local Life

Santana's A-Frame Houses

Santana (Map p74, E3) is known for its A-frame houses, built with thatched roofs reaching the ground to protect from the north's inclement weather. Santana's tourist office is housed in a specially built example. Head to Rua João Abel de Freitas, where the owner of an original structure lets people wander round for a small donation.

Funchal. (www.parquetematicodamadeira. pt; Estrada Regional 101, Santana; adult/child €10/8; ⊙10am-7pm mid-Jun–mid-Sep & mid-Dec–mid-Jan, closed Mon other times)

Igreja do Bom Jesus CHURCH

5 ⊙ Map p74, C3

The fishing village of Ponta Delgada, 30km west of Santana, is worth a brief halt for its authentic remoteness and to visit the baroque Igreja do Bom Jesus. The church houses an 18th-century crucifix that mysteriously washed ashore in 1740. It's the focus of the local Festa de Senhor Jesus, a few days in September when Ponta Delgada awakes from its slumber. (Ponta Delgada)

Porta da Cruz VILLAGE

6 ⊙ Map p74, E4

The easternmost point you can reach on this coast before mammoth cliffs persuade the road to head inland, Porta da Cruz is a picturesque spot nestling at the base of some seriously steep terraced slopes. From March to May

Madeira's last working sugar mill fills the village with a sweet scent.

Eating

Quinta do Furão INTERNATIONAL €€

7 ✕ Map p74, E3

Stylishly rustic, this hotel-restaurant sets the highest standards on the north coast. Wonderfully imaginative gourmet dishes, such as cream of beetroot soup with glazed chestnuts, foie gras infused with Madeira wine and quail marinated in sugar-cane molasses blend international familiarity with a touch of exotic Macaronesia. The terrace offers astonishing views. (www.quintadofurao.com; Achada do Gramacho, Santana; mains €9-17; ⊙noon-9.30pm)

Cantinho da Serra MADEIRAN €€

8 ✕ Map p74, E3

Located a five-minute drive from Santana heading towards Achada do Teixeira, this rustic inn creates a cosy atmosphere with its real log fires, hearty traditional Madeiran food and country decor. Meals are served in clay pots keeping the *bacalhau* (salt cod), lamb, goat and fish piping hot. The wines are mostly mainland affairs. (www.cantinhodaserra.com; Estrada do Pico das Pedras, Santana; mains €9-17; ⊙12.30-10pm)

Estrela do Norte MADEIRAN €€

9 ✕ Map p74, E3

The 'Northern Star' seats 145 at formally laid, tightly packed tables, onto which

waitstaff plonk the mainstays of
Madeiran cuisine, such as *espada* (scabbard fish) with banana, *espetada* (grilled
beef skewers) and marinated pork. If
you've had your fill of regional cuisine,
there are also decent pizzas and house
specials. (Avenida Manuel Marques Trinidade
24, Santana; mains €7-14; ⏱10am-10pm)

Cachelote
MADEIRAN €€

10 ✖ Map p74, A2

The recently revamped 'Whale' wins the
prize for Madeira's craziest restaurant
location, sitting atop the crumbly
volcanic rock on Port Moniz seafront,
occasionally taking a wave from the furious Atlantic. Inside you'll discover an
exhibition on the town's whaling and
agricultural past before you reach the
dining room and plates of marinated
pork and *espada*. (Rua Forte de São João Batista, Porto Moniz; mains €9-17; ⏱noon-11pm)

Quebra Mar
MADEIRAN €€

11 ✖ Map p74, B3

Located on the São Vicente seafront,
the town's best restaurant serves up
360-degree views of the coast and
seascape (the dining room actually
revolves slowly), as well as meat and
fish in equal measure, focusing firmly
on Madeiran mainstays such as scabbard, *espetada,* tuna and fish stew. For
dessert, go for the *pudim de veludo*
(custard and caramel pudding). (☎291
842 338; www.restaurantequebramar.com;
Sítio do Calhau, São Vicente; mains €8-16;
⏱9am-6pm Mon, to 10pm Tue-Sun)

Churrascaria Santana
PORTUGUESE €

Gourmets will shun this smoky local
grill (see 9 ✖ Map p74, E3) but this is
a superb spot to meet day-tripping
families, forestry workers and Santana's police force over slabs of cheap
grilled meat and Portuguese reds.
Tables are nicely laid with chequered
tablecloths and the welcome is friendly.
(Avenida Manuel Marques Trindade, Santana;
mains €8-11.50; ⏱10am-10pm)

Ferro Velho
MADEIRAN €

12 ✖ Map p74, B3

A long-standing pub-restaurant in the
cobbled streets of old São Vicente, this
is the best place to cradle a Coral in
the evenings if you're not driving back
to the capital. Bedecked with football
scarves and number plates from around
the world, the food here is cheap
but it's best to stick to the typically
Madeiran menu items. (Rua da Fonte Velha,
São Vicente; mains €3-9; ⏱11am-11pm)

Local Life
Former North Coast Road

Road number 101 once struck fear
into the heart of every Madeiran
driver until it was retired to Room
101 by the modern VE2. The old
route was the island's most dramatic road, the barely car-wide
strip of tarmac clinging to the side
of cliffs and splashed by waterfalls
and waves. Some sections (one-way
towards Porto Moniz) are still open.

Local Life
Drive through Eastern Madeira

Getting There

🚗 The route starts in Funchal but not on the Via Rápida. Instead head north from the city centre following signposts to Monte, the first stop.

This drive around Madeira's eastern half takes in mountain vistas, sleepy coastal villages and some fine spots to sample local fare. Best done in your own hire car, so you can spend as much or as little time as you like at each stop, the route should take the best part of a whole day to complete if stopping everywhere.

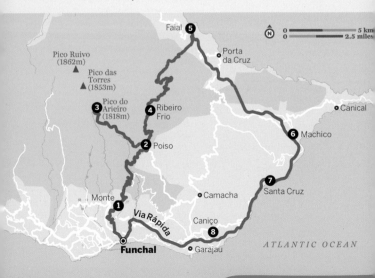

1 Monte

You might have already seen Monte's attractions (p68), but a second visit can be a completely different experience – at 500m above sea level, Madeira's fickle weather can change dramatically up here, wreathing the Igreja da Nossa Senhora and Largo da Fonte in dense fog or bathing them in Atlantic rays.

2 Poiso

From Monte, it's an almost vertical drive north to Poiso, where the cosy inn Casa de Abrigo do Poiso (p111) stands at the turn-off for Madeira's third-highest peak, Pico do Arieiro. It's a nice spot for a midmorning *chinesa* (milky coffee) and *pastel de nata* (custard tart).

3 Pico do Arieiro

The drive to the top of Pico do Arieiro takes you well above the tree line and ends at the radar station, cafe, souvenir shop and very steep car park that crowd around the summit. On a clear day the views from here are simply stupendous.

4 Ribeiro Frio

The only way from Pico do Arieiro is down, back to Poiso, from where it's around 15 minutes of up-down driving to the nippy village of Ribeiro Frio. Restaurants here serve local trout, which can be seen chasing each other in endless circles at the trout farm (p110).

5 Faial

Cowering picturesquely under the Penha D'Águia (Eagle's Rock), a massive hulk of rock rising almost 600 vertical metres from the Atlantic, the north-coast village of Faial is a sleepy, undervisited place with a pretty church. The only time things come to life here is during the annual Festa da Anona (Custard Apple Festival) in late February/early March.

6 Machico

Take the fast road through several tunnels to lively Machico, Madeira's second 'city', former capital and the spot captain Zarco first stepped ashore to claim Madeira for Portugal (there's a small plaque at the harbour). The town has several undemanding sights, an artificial beach and some good restaurants, such as Maré Alta (p86).

7 Santa Cruz

As the village at the end of Madeira airport's runway, the most memorable thing about Santa Cruz might be the sight of planes gliding low over the rocky beach as they attempt to hit the tarmac and not the briny.

8 Caniço & Caniço de Baixo

Now virtually attached to Funchal by urban sprawl, Caniço has a tiny historical centre boasting an attractive church and the Quinta Splendida Gardens. Head downhill to quieter Caniço de Baixo to watch the sunset from the suntrap bathing area of Complexo Balnear Lido Galomar (p132).

Explore

East Madeira

Outside Funchal, east Madeira is the island's most heavily populated area with the 'second city' and former capital Machico, Madeira's main port at Caniçal and the island's stilt-walking airport all at this end. It's an action-packed area of gliding Boeings and aqua parks, golden sand and stupendous views, all just a short ride from Funchal along the Via Rápida.

The Region in a Day

☼ It's just possible to see most of eastern Madeira's sights in a day by bus, but of course it's far easier by car. Some 700m higher than Funchal seafront, Camacha is known for its wicker and the **factory** (p82) here should be your first stop. From here you could head down to the airport to spot **planes** (p85) making the dramatic approach over the Atlantic, or push on to Machico (pictured left), where a beach of golden sand and a fish lunch at **Maré Alta** (p86) awaits.

☼ One of Madeira's best museums is the **Museu da Baleia** (p85) in Caniçal, where you can learn everything you ever wanted to know about whales and Madeira's long-defunct whaling industry. It's a fascinating place and count on spending over two hours here. Stalls on the seafront sell scrimshaw – whale-bone art.

☾ Come evening you might want to double back to Machico, which has the liveliest seafront away from Funchal, or to Caniço for a dinner of grilled meat at **A Central** (p86). In summer watch a memorable sunset from the **Cristo Rei** (p85) statue in Garajau.

👁 Top Experiences

Camacha Wicker Factory (p82)

🖤 Best of East Madeira

Eating

Maré Alta (p86)

La Perla (p86)

Museums

Museu da Baleia (p85)

Walks

Ponta de São Lourenço hike (p122)

Beaches

Praia de Machico (p132)

Praia de Garajau (p132)

Complexo Balnear Lido Galomar (p132)

Getting There

🚗 **Car** For full flexibility, the best way to see the sights of the east coast is by car.

🚌 **Bus** The following buses serve east Madeira from Funchal: Machico, SAM buses 20, 23, 53, 78 and 113; Camacha, Horários do Funchal bus 129; Caniço, many eastbound SAM buses; Caniçal, SAM bus 113; Aeroporto da Madeira, SAM Airport bus, plus many Machico services.

Top Experiences
Camacha Wicker Factory

Apart from being well-known among Portuguese sports fans as the venue for the first ever football match in Portugal (there's a monument in the main square), Camacha today is all about one traditional product – wicker. Harvested in the mountains around the town, it's dried and graded before being twisted and weaved into myriad objects of varying degrees of usefulness. The epicentre of the Madeiran wicker industry is a building in the centre of town called O Relógio (the Clock).

👁 Map p84, B3

📞 291 922 777

Largo Conselheiro Aires de Ornelas 12, Camacha

admission free

🕑 8.45am-6pm

Handicrafts on display at Camacha Wicker Factory

Don't Miss

Basket Cases

This being Madeira, O Relógio is entered high up on the 2nd floor, where you'll find the shop. Half exhibition, half souvenir emporium, the wicker comes in all shapes and sizes, from huge mirror frames and doll's house furniture to suitcases and bread baskets, mini Monte toboggans and lampshades to fruit baskets and wine-bottle holders. Prices are very reasonable and the quality extremely high – items often last for decades.

Weird & Wonderful World of Wicker

Down a level from the shop, an exhibition of wicker creations will have you reaching for your camera. A wicker replica of Zarco's caravel sails towards the stairs while basket monkeys and frogs stare back at you with old-fashioned teddy-bear eyes. You won't be reaching for your wallet here, though – no matter how much you offer, sadly none of this is for sale. What you can buy are the large pieces of furniture, very popular among Madeira's smaller guest houses and *quinta* (mansion) hotels.

Fabrica

Arguably the most interesting part of O Relógio is the basement where four or five nimble-fingered local craftspeople sit on old cushions creating items for the shop. They'll gladly demonstrate their skill and let you handle the items they make, but few speak any English. Here you can also see the crude wooden templates they use to fashion baskets and lampshades, as well as inspect the bushels of graded wicker stacked up against the walls.

☑ Top Tips

▶ The town is 700m above sea level meaning the weather is invariably cooler here than in Funchal. Many are caught out by this.

▶ The shop can ship furniture to your home address, but nothing smaller.

▶ Horários do Funchal bus 129 from Funchal is the best way to get here; there's more choice going back.

▶ The viewing terrace behind O Relógio has amazing views 700m down to the Atlantic.

▶ Kids will enjoy the large playground on the square in front of O Relógio.

✗ Take a Break

O Relógio (Largo Conselieiro Aires de Ornelas, Camacha; mains €7.50-14.50; ⏱noon-4pm Nov-Mar, noon-4pm & 7-10pm Apr-Oct), above the wicker shop and factory, is the best option for a full meal. The cafe next to the shop has cakes, coffees and sandwiches.

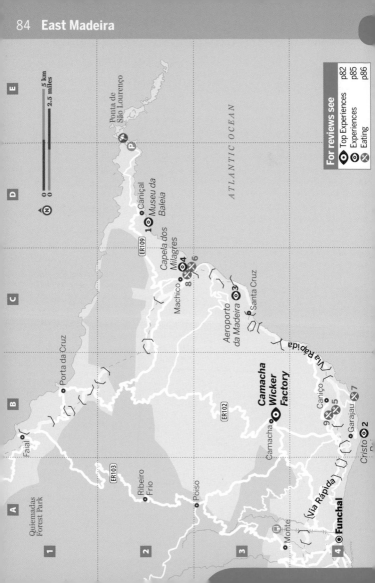

E

D

C

B

A

1

2

3

4

0   5 km
0   2.5 miles

N

ATLANTIC OCEAN

Ponta de
São Lourenço

Caniçal
● Museu da
Baleia
1

ER109

Capela dos
Milagres
4
6

Machico ●
8

Santa Cruz
3

Aeroporto
da Madeira

Via Rápida

Porta da Cruz ●

ER102

**Camacha
Wicker Factory**

Caniço
9 **5**
7

Garajau ●
Cristo **2**

Faial ●

ER103

Ribeiro
Frio ●

Poiso ●

Monte ●

Funchal

(Via Rápida)

Quiemadas
Forest Park

For reviews see

◆ Top Experiences p82
◉ Experiences p85
✗ Eating p86

Experiences

Museu da Baleia
MUSEUM

1 ⊙ Map p84, D2

Once a minor exhibition, Caniçal's Whale Museum moved to a large, multi-million-euro ultramodern complex in 2012, making it possibly the world's best museum devoted to the topic. The fascinating museum is divided into two sections – whaling on Madeira and whales – with an automatic commentary playing in your ears as you go. (www.museudabaleia.org; Rua Garcia Moniz 1, Caniçal; adult/child incl audio-guide €10/5; ⊙11am-6pm Tue-Sun Mar-Oct, 10am-5pm Nov-Feb)

Cristo Rei, Garajau

Cristo Rei
STATUE

2 ⊙ Map p84, B4

The upmarket village of Garajau hangs for dear life on the side of a cliff, 6km as the crow flies from central Funchal. On an often blustery promontory below the village stands the *Cristo Rei,* a late-1920s mini-version of Rio's *Christ the Redeemer* statue, arms outspread, eyes gazing into the infinite blue of the Atlantic. (Estrada Nova de Cristo Rei, Garajau)

Aeroporto da Madeira
LANDMARK

3 ⊙ Map p84, C3

Few airports could be counted as true places of interest, but Madeira's runway sticking out on stilts into the Atlantic and surrounded on three sides by mountains definitely can be. From Santa Cruz head uphill along the ER207 which runs high above the runway for great views of planes performing the tricky landing manoeuvre. (www.ana.pt; Santa Cruz)

Capela dos Milagres
CHAPEL

4 ⊙ Map p84, C2

Machico has three churches but the most famous is the pretty little Miracles Chapel on the north side of the river. It was famously washed away in a flood in 1803, but the crucifix was found bobbing in the Atlantic by an American galley. 'Miracle!' the locals declared, hence the chapel's name. (Rua do Senhor dos Milagres, Machico)

Eating

La Perla
INTERNATIONAL €€€

5 ✖ Map p84, B4

Occupying the original 19th-century mansion house at the Quinta Splendida, this gourmet restaurant serves the most exquisite meals on this stretch of coast. Take a seat in one of the three rooms to enjoy a seasonal menu, with the flambéed dishes a speciality of the house. For dessert, go for the crêpes Suzette, flambéed with Grand Marnier and orange sauce. (www.quintasplendida. com; Estrada da Ponta Oliveira 11, Caniço; menu €60, mains €15-30; ⏰7-10pm Wed, Fri & Sun)

Maré Alta
SEAFOOD €€

6 ✖ Map p84, C3

This seafront glass box contains Machico's best seafood restaurant. Every inhabitant of Madeira's waters, plus many from elsewhere, swim in shoals through the menu, which includes local limpets, tuna, *espada* (scabbard fish), octopus and imported shellfish. (Largo da Praça, Machico; mains €11.50-20; ⏰11am-11pm)

Understand
The Machin Legend

Some claim Machico is named after Robert Machin, a 14th-century Bristol merchant who was washed up here while eloping with his lover Anne of Hertford. The 'discoverer' of Madeira, captain Zarco, is supposed to have stumbled across their graves when first stepping ashore.

Atlantis
MADEIRAN €€

7 ✖ Map p84, B4

The aptly named Atlantis looks as though it's risen from the waves and clamped itself to the cliffside above the suntrap beach below the Galomar Hotel. Seating options are on chunky wicker inside or on the terrace above the crashing Atlantic. You'd expect an exclusively seafood menu, but meat and even uncommon dishes such as duck make an appearance. (☎291 930 930; Ponta D'Oliveira, Caniço de Baixo; mains €11.50-14; ⏰10am-10pm)

Mercado Velho
MADEIRAN €€

8 ✖ Map p84, C2

Ensconced in the old market building, this long-established restaurant just back from the seafront has a pretty outdoor seating area gathered around the old market sinks, as well as a more formal indoor space. The eclectic menu includes meat and fish, as well as pizzas, soups and salads. (Rua do Mercado, Machico; mains €9-18; ⏰10am-11pm)

A Central
PORTUGUESE, BRAZILIAN €€

9 ✖ Map p84, B4

A smoky aroma wafts from the door of this central Caniço *churrascaria* (traditional grill). Meat and fish, expertly barbecued on acacia cinders and served with salad and wine, is the deal here. The *rodizio brasileiro* – 14 types of skewered meat – sorts the carnivores from the boys. (Rua João Paulo II 10-14, Caniço; mains €8-14; ⏰11am-2am)

Understand

Protecting Madeira's Natural Habitats

Gregory Peck types harpooned their way around it, ship-builders stripped it of hard wood and captain Zarco is even said to have set fire to the whole caboodle to clear the land for wheat production – humans have hardly been good news for the island of Madeira, but these days protection, replanting and conservation are slowly returning things to the way they were six centuries ago.

Once covering large tracts of southern Europe, the *laurisilva* (forests of laurel and cedar) were completely wiped out on the continent by the last ice age but survived in Macaronesia (Madeira, Canary Islands, Azores). Placed on Unesco's list of World Heritage Sites in 1999, the 150 sq km of woodland is Madeira's most valued natural habitat, largely confined to the inaccessible valleys and mountains of the north and north-west. The Centro Ciência Viva (p75) in Porto Moniz is the best place to learn more about this remnant of primeval forest. Queimadas Forest Park near Santana is a good place to immerse yourself in the real thing.

Though the pines and eucalyptus trees planted in the mid-20th century for timber look and smell good, they are alien species and are gradually being replaced with indigenous laurels, bay trees, juniper and ironwood. Commercial forestry is also being gradually phased out.

Conservation efforts are also in full swing out at sea. The Garajau's Marine Reserve on the south coast was created in 1986 in an area where whales were once hauled onto the shore and dismembered. The waters around Garajau are particularly rich in underwater life and have become a popular diving site.

Of course, Madeira is not alone in this part of the Atlantic – dominating the horizon 35km from Funchal are the uninhabited Desertas, the three elongated islands forming one large nature reserve. In 1989, the Desertas monk seal was one of the world's most endangered species, with just eight animals left. There are now around 30 and numbers are expected to grow rapidly over the coming decades. The three Selvagens Islands 280km south of Madeira were declared a nature reserve as early as 1971, mostly due to their bird populations.

Special Feature

Levada Paths

One of the reasons people come to Madeira is to hike the levadas – 2500km of irrigation channels along which lead gentle paths through the wilds. A levada walk is the quintessential Madeira experience – depart Funchal early in the morning, wander the dramatic landscape, picnicking along the way, and make it back into the city for dinner. Try at least one – most visitors are hooked straightaway.

Don't Miss

Going it Alone

There aren't many levada walks you can't tackle on your own. However, accessing the start of the trail can take some planning, especially if you don't have a hire car. All of Madeira's bus companies now post their timetables online and routes are designed with tourists and walkers in mind. The tourist office in Funchal can help out with planning, as can hotel receptions. Doing things by car creates a problem as levada walks are linear routes, meaning you might need a bus to get you back to where you parked. Taxis are a good solution but can make the day an expensive affair. For example, if you arrange for a Funchal cab to wait in Portela, the trip back to the city costs €50.

Joining a Group

Every day tens of groups leave for the levadas on half- and full-day hikes. While these free you of the need to think about the logistics of getting to and from the walk, groups often move fast and you don't have the freedom to tarry where you like for as long as you like. Tours are cheap (around €25 for a full-day hike), guides usually very clued up and you are often picked up and dropped off at your accommodation by the tour company. However groups can be large, clogging up the narrow paths and scaring off wildlife. Cruise-ship groups can be particularly huge. Lunch is sometimes provided for an extra charge and bookings can be made at countless places throughout the Hotel Zone.

Maps & Guidebooks

If you are heading out alone, having a map and/ or specialist guidebook is recommended. The Sunflower guides to Madeira by John and Pat

Getting There

🚌 **Bus** Levada walks are normally accessible by bus, though this is not always the case.

🚕 **Taxi** Many walkers arrange for a taxi to wait at the end of the route to return them to Funchal.

☑ Top Tips

▶ It's often a good idea to contact the tourist office to find out if the route you intend to take is affected by the weather or repair work.

▶ Good hiking boots, a torch, waterproofs and food are a must.

▶ Exposed sections are common and definitely not for vertigo sufferers.

▶ Never walk in the levadas, throw anything into them or (how should we put it?) use them as an outdoor convenience.

✕ Take a Break

Taking a break on the levadas is simple – pack a picnic. There are precious few eating options on the paths themselves.

Underwood set the standard for all the others and are widely available on the island (even at supermarkets in the Hotel Zone). *Levadas and Footpaths of Madeira* by Raimundo Quintal is a little out of date but gives a lot of background. Cicerone's *Walking in Madeira* maps out 60 routes across the island while *Walk Madeira* by Shirley and Mike Whitehead plots a range of hikes for all abilities. *Madeira Tour and Trail* 1:40,000 available on Madeira is one of the best maps around. Kompass sheet 234 *Madeira* 1:50,000 is also a good companion on the trails and when driving.

Understand
Story of the Levadas

Many countries around the world have created irrigation systems but none are quite like Madeira's levadas. Apart from being a feat of engineering, determination and ingenuity, it's their accessibility and the truly spectacular landscapes to which they give access that make them truly unique. They are the lifeblood of the island, providing water to taps, fields and gardens, and electricity to homes and businesses through hydroelectric power – with no real stable rivers, without them human habitation on Madeira would be nigh on impossible.

So how did such a small island come to have such a mammoth network of levadas? The first settlers soon realised that the rainfall and mist that drenched the mountainous interior somehow needed to be channelled down to the warm, dry south coast. Over 2m of precipitation a year can fall in the north of the island while the fertile south coast may not see a drop for half a year. Work began in the 16th-century on creating fast-flowing aqueducts and over the next three centuries the network was developed, often using slave labour. Many died carving out the channels through impossibly rugged mountainscapes but by the 1900s, 1000km of levadas were supplying water for agriculture and for drinking.

But there was a problem – many levadas were privately owned and the distribution of precious water was often unfair. In 1939 the state stepped in to study the irrigation system and commission more channels. By 1970 the system was essentially complete, though minor work is still ongoing. The island's longest levadas such as the Levada do Norte and the Levada dos Tornos were built at this time and are vital pieces of infrastructure.

As you enjoy a leisurely levada stroll, spare a thought for those who maintain the hundreds of kilometres of channels, tunnels, bridges, reservoirs, ducts and sluices. Around 99% of the system can only be accessed on foot – tools and materials have to be hauled by teams of workers sometimes tens of kilometres to where a rock fall or a landslip has caused a snarl-up. You will often meet these hardy work gangs on the trails.

Top: Farmland around
Ribeiro Frio (p92)

Right: Wooden house along
Caldeirão Verde trail (p95),
Queimadas Forest Park

RAINER MIRAU/GETTY IMAGES ©

Local Life
Levada Walk:
Ribeiro Frio to Portela

One of the best and most easily accessible levada walks on the island, this classic route runs from chilly Ribeiro Frio through some rip-roaringly spectacular landscapes, across the sides of sheer cliffs and through the thick Unesco-protected laurisilva forest ending 11km (around four hours) later at Portela, with the often fast-flowing Levada do Furado accompanying you most of the way.

❶ Ribeiro Frio

Horários do Funchal buses 56 and 103 drop you off at the Restaurante Ribeiro Frio, behind which you will find the beginning of the Levada do Furado – the path is signposted PR10. This is one of the oldest levadas constructed by the state and dates back to 1822. It was created to irrigate farmland around Porto da Cruz.

Views towards Penha D'Águia (Eagle's Rock)

2 Ribeira do Poço do Bezerro

After an hour the bridge where the Levada do Furado is joined by another levada is a good place to stop for lunch, if you've timed things right. It's a lovely spot with the sound of gurgling water, rustling trees and birdsong all around. The finches here are so tame, they will eat out of your hand.

3 Through the Rocks

After around 1¼ hours the path and levada pass through a huge cleft in the rock. From the outside it looks as though you might need a torch to pass through but this isn't the case. Follow the stepping stones until your reach the other end.

4 Cabeça Furado

Things get very tight after around two hours when the levada and the path squeeze onto a ledge cut out of the Suna escarpment. Some parts here are pretty exposed and you need to watch your footing. The views out across the chasm are dizzyingly spectacular. For many this section is the levada hiking they had in mind predeparture.

5 Lamaceiros

After around 2¾ hours you should reach the Lamaceiros forestry station from where you should be able to see the Ponta de São Lourenço. From here it's all downhill with more spectacular views. The landscape also changes as the thick tree cover gives way to fields. The going is very easy from here.

6 Levada da Portela

The Levada do Furado ends at Lamaceiros and you now pick up the Levada da Portela, either a gurgling rush of water or a dry concrete channel, depending on where water is needed. On the way down, it's not difficult to spot the massive Penha D'Águia (Eagle's Rock) and the village of Faial on the north coast.

7 Portela

The descent into Portela passes the reservoir that stores the levada's water for future distribution. When you reach the road at the end of the path, turn left for Portela. SAM buses 53 and 78 make the trip back to Funchal, though you should look up the timetable beforehand as the service is sporadic and a taxi back to the capital quite expensive.

Local Life
Levada Walk:
Levada do Caldeirão Verde

A popular levada, the PR9 route is one of the most picturesque on Madeira, running for 6.5km (plus 6.5km back) through show-stopping landscapes. The levada pushes through some impossible territory, clinging to the sides of vertical rock faces and burrowing through tunnels. A torch is essential for this hike – you might also want to bring your swimwear for a dip at the end.

❶ Getting to the Start
To reach the start at Queimadas, take any of the three morning Horários do Funchal number 56 buses to Santana, then a taxi. If you're up for it and have made an early start, the walk from Santana is around 4km but it's mostly uphill and quite tiring in hot conditions.

Queimadas Forest Park

❷ Queimadas Forest Park

Some 990m above sea level, Queimadas is a delightful spot, with half-timbered forestry rest houses surrounding a duck pond amid a sea of verdant moss and ferns, the cut pebble paths lined with the gnarled fences of heath tree branches, common across the island. Two popular walking routes depart from here. One to Caldeirão Verde, the other to Pico das Pedras.

❸ Two Ravines

From Queimadas a red clay path (slippery in wet conditions) runs along the levada. The first major obstacle the water course has to tackle are two ravines formed by the Ribeira dos Cedros and the Ribeira da Fonte do Louro. Shortly after these are behind you comes the first short tunnel (around the one-hour mark).

❹ Flora Spotting

This is one of the most remote locations on Madeira meaning there's a lot of flora to identify along the way. Japanese cedars, red European beech, juniper, broom heath and Madeira blueberry are just some of the species to look out for. You are also passing through the laurisilva forest, a Unesco-protected remnant of the woodland that once covered southern Europe.

❺ Channel Tunnels

Three more tunnels follow in quick succession, so now is the time to get the torch out. The longest is the second one, which also includes a bend, so you can't see the end at the beginning. Watch your footwork as the floors are uneven, shine the torch about 5m in front of you and keep your head down.

❻ Birdwatching

Bird life is the other nature-spotter's highlight along this route. As on other levada walks, chaffinches have learnt which side their *bolo do caco* is buttered and will tamely eat from your outstretched palm. Others to look out for are the long-toed pigeon, the firecrest, the grey wagtail and the buzzard.

❼ Caldeirão Verde

A short distance from the last tunnel, the Caldeirão Verde appears to the left. The 'Green Cauldron' is one of the prettiest spots on the island of Madeira: a waterfall gushing into a lake from a height of around 100m and encircled by a tall amphitheatre of plant life. It's a magic experience if you find yourself here alone.

❽ Going Further

From Caldeirão Verde you can simply retrace your steps back to Queimadas or, if you are feeling adventurous, carry on to the Caldeirão do Inferno, a deep chasm between two peaks reached through numerous tunnels, before returning to Quiemadas the way you came.

Local Life
Levada Walk: Rabaçal – Levada do Risco & Levada das 25 Fontes

On the southern edge of the Paúl da Serra, Rabaçal is the starting point for hikes that are some of the most popular among tour groups and locals – in fact it's one of the few levadas on which you might meet day-tripping Funchalese. This watery wonderland of springs and waterfalls is the point where three levadas converge. This walk takes in two of them, with a total return distance of around 16km.

1 Getting There

There's simply no way to reach Rabaçal by public transport as no bus serves the ER110 road across the uninhabited Paúl da Serra. Organising a ride from Calheta works out cheapest, otherwise you'll have to hire a car. The road to Rabaçal from the ER110 is closed to traffic, so you have to park and walk down.

Hiker near Rabaçal

❷ Rabaçal

Trail PR6 (Levada das 25 Fontes) and PR6.1 (Levada do Risco) both start at Rabaçal (1064m), the combined hiking distance of around 16km making a great day out. Starting at the Rabaçal houses, take the highest levada, the Levada do Risco. After about 30 minutes you should pass a fork in the path, the other route leading to 25 Fontes.

❸ Risco Waterfall

It only takes around another 10 minutes to hike to this wonderful waterfall that plunges from a height of 100m into a lagoon. It's a romantic spot, especially if you can time a visit to avoid the tour groups that head this way. It's also probably time for lunch and there's no better spot on the island to unpack supplies.

❹ Diverse Habitats

Natural habitats vary at this height above sea level. Moorland dominates, but there are also areas of laurisilva forest. Broom heath thrives here, as does Madeiran whortleberry. The endemic Trocaz pigeon nests in these parts, easy to spot thanks to the zebra stripes on its neck.

❺ Ribeira Grande

Head back the way you came for 10 minutes until you reach the fork again. This time take the Levada das 25 Fontes. After 20 minutes you cross the riverbed of the Ribeira Grande, after which the channel narrows down considerably with drops on your left. Take care on this section.

❻ 25 Fontes

In around 30 minutes you should reach the 25 Fontes, another pool fed by numerous (though possibly not 25) waterfalls. Legend has it that anyone who submerges themselves in the lagoon will never resurface. Water from here eventually finds its way to the hydroelectric power station in Calheta. From here retrace your steps back to Rabaçal.

❼ Further Exploration

Few attempt the third hike from Rabaçal along the Levada da Rocha Vermelha, which sees none of the tour groups that clog the other two paths. The route has a very remote feel as you head into the island's interior above the valley of Madeira's longest river, the Ribeira da Janela.

Explore

West Madeira

West of Funchal is where the Madeiran sun shines brightest, with long light-filled days, dramatic sunsets and millions of the island's sweet miniature bananas and Malvasia grapes ripening in the heat. Varied and scenically dramatic, there's a lot to see and do off the slow road west, from the fishing traditions of Câmara de Lobos to the cutting-edge art of Calheta.

The Region in a Day

☀ As with other parts of the island, you'll need a car to see everything in a long day. Take the slow road from Funchal's Hotel Zone to **Câmara de Lobos** (p102; pictured left), to perhaps see the last of the village's fishers bringing in the catch. From there take the Via Rápida (south coast road) to delightful Ribeira Brava for a look around the **Museu Etnográfico da Madeira** (p101) and lunch on the seafront at **Borda D'Agua** (p103).

☀ Back on the road, your next stop is Calheta and its unexpectedly striking **Casa das Mudas** (p102) gallery of contemporary art. Still in Calheta, drive down to the artificial beach for a dip in the Atlantic and a coffee.

☾ One of the best places to watch the spectacular Atlantic sunset is Madeira's most westerly point, **Ponta do Pargo** (p102). Park the car in the village and head along the trail that leads to the lighthouse, where hopefully the sun and the ocean will oblige in a riot of colour.

♥ **Best of West Madeira**

Museums
Museu Etnográfico da Madeira (p101)

For Free
Cabo Girão (p101)

Beaches
Praia da Calheta (p132)
Piscinas Naturais (p132)

Villages
Ponta do Sol (p133)
Ribeira Brava (p133)
Paúl do Mar (p133)

Getting There

🚌 **Bus** The following Rodoeste buses serve the west of the island from Funchal: Ribeira Brava, bus 7; Calheta, bus 139; Câmara de Lobos, most west-bound buses; Cabo Girão, bus 7; Ponta do Pargo, bus 100/142.

ER107

Curral das Freiras

ER104

Encumeada Pass

São Vicente

Central Valley

VE1

Central Valley

ER110

Serra de Água

VE4

Jardim da Serra

⊗6

Museu Etnográfico da Madeira

Câmara de Lobos

⊚4

⊚2

Cabo Girão

9 1 ⊙⊙ 3
⊗⊗
8

Igreja de São Bento

Ribeira Brava

ER110

Madalena do Mar

Ponta do Sol

Calheta

⊙⊙5
7

Casa das Mudas

ATLANTIC OCEAN

ER110

ER101

Paúl do Mar

A

Ponta do Pargo

For reviews see

⊙ Experiences   p101
⊗ Eating   p102

0   10 km
0   5 miles

⊛ N

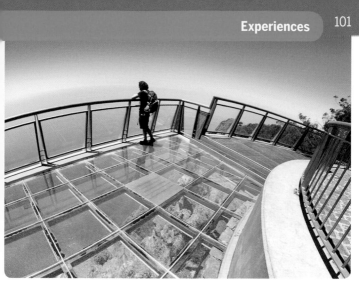

Cabo Girão viewing platform

Experiences

Museu Etnográfico da Madeira

MUSEUM

1 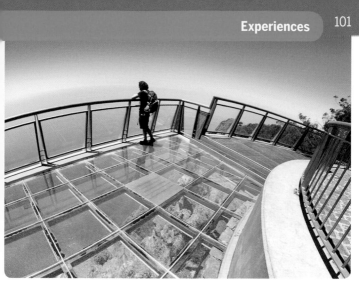 Map p100, D3

One of Madeira's best museums, the collections here look at every aspect of the island's traditional life, from *espada* (scabbard fish) fishing to wicker weaving, and wine production to toboggan transport. There's an old shop complete with till nostalgically still taking *escudos*, live weaving demonstrations and fascinating temporary exhibitions to inspect. (Rua de São Francisco 24, Ribeira Brava; adult/child €3/free; 9.30am-5pm Tue-Fri, 10am-12.30pm & 1.30-5.30pm Sat)

Cabo Girão

VIEWPOINT

2 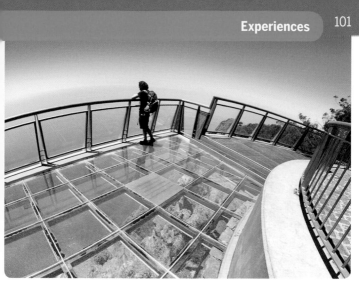 Map p100, E4

Around 3km west of Câmara de Lobos, Madeira's highest sea cliffs rise 580m over the village and the Atlantic's sapphire expanse. Some of the highest sea cliffs in Europe, the panorama from the viewing platform is spectacular. Spectacular that is, unless you look down – the new platform floor is made of glass and hangs over the cliff edge – a knee-weakening, toe-curling experience! (24hr)

Igreja de São Bento

CHURCH

3 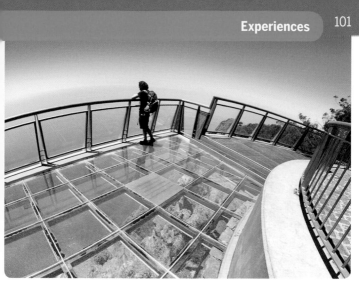 Map p100, D4

Originally dating from the 15th century, this attractive church occupies a pebble

 Local Life
Ponta do Pargo

Madeira's most westerly point is **Ponta do Pargo** (Map p100, A1; Red Snapper Point). From the village, a 2km trail heads up to a lighthouse from where there are spectacular Atlantic vistas – an especially good spot to find yourself at sundown.

square in the very centre of Ribeira Brava. Almost as wide as it is long, the three-nave interior is divided by high Gothic arches, which reach up to a curved, embossed ceiling. From this hang the church's most impressive feature, two giant crystal chandeliers. (www.igrejarbrava.com; Rua dos Camachos, Ribeira Brava; ⊙8am-6pm Mon-Sat, from 7am Sun)

Câmara de Lobos
VILLAGE

4 ◉ Map p100, E4

Every visitor to Funchal at some point finds themselves in this adjoining fishing village, whether at the end of a hike, on an open-top bus, coming down from Cabo Girão or on an island tour. It's the centre of Madeira's traditional fishing industry, with the colourful boats hauled up in the little harbour by day, the rough-and-ready fisherfolk occupying many tiny bars. (www.cm-camaradelobos.pt; Câmara de Lobos)

Casa das Mudas
GALLERY

5 ◉ Map p100, B2

Housed in an almost Minecraft-like building above Calheta, this contem-

porary arts space has a gallery, shop, cafe, auditorium and workshop area. It's worth the climb from the beach for the changing exhibitions or just to ogle Paulo David's dramatic architectural achievement. (Estrada Simão Gonçalves da Câmara 37, Calheta; admission €5; ⊙10am-6pm Tue-Sun)

Eating

Vila do Peixe
SEAFOOD €€

This contemporary restaurant is the best in Câmara de Lobos (see 4 ◉ Map p100, E4). It offers the highest quality Madeiran fish and seafood. The fish, including parrot fish, red bream, *dourada* (sea bream) and *espada* are sold by weight, lightly salted and grilled to perfection on acacia embers. Local seafood include limpets, whelks and occasionally octopus. Wednesday is folklore night, Friday fado evening. Free shuttle bus from any hotel. (☎291 099 909; www.viladopeixe.com; Rua Dr João Abel de Freitas 30A, Câmara de Lobos; mains €5-15; ⊙noon-11pm)

Quinta da Serra
INTERNATIONAL €€€

6 ✖ Map p100, E3

The French chef at this luxury hotel restaurant in the settlement of Jardim da Serra cooks up an imaginative, international menu using only organic ingredients – a first for Madeira. The dining room is an elegant affair and the service is impeccable. (☎291 640 120; www.hotelquintadaserra.com; Estrada do Chote 4/6, Jardim da Serra; ⊙1-3pm & 6.30-10pm)

Vila da Carne PORTUGUESE €€

Vila do Peixe's sister restaurant (see 4 ⊙ Map p100, E4) is the 'House of Meat' a clean-cut eatery specialising in *espetada* done in the traditional way (chunks of beef covered in salt, garlic and laurel leaf, impaled on a green laurel skewer and grilled over acacia embers). Interesting sides include sweet potatoes with molasses and typical Madeiran *milho frito* (fried corn cubes). (Rua Dr João Abel Freitas 30, Câmara de Lobos; mains €9-14; ⊙noon-11pm)

Convento das Vinhas MADEIRAN, INTERNATIONAL €€

7 ✕ Map p100, B2

Perched high above Calheta, this family-run place serves up excellent food with a hefty side of panoramic views. Madeiran and international favourites pack the menu, but this is possibly the only place on Madeira where you can order a local delicacy – *ovas de espada* – scabbard-fish eggs. (Caminho Lombo do Salão 35, Calheta; mains €7-13; ⊙11am-11pm Mon-Sat, to 10pm Sun)

Borda D'Agua PORTUGUESE €€

8 ✕ Map p100, D3

Right on the seafront as the name suggests, this multitasking eatery can serve as a lunchtime quickie for coffee and sandwiches outside, or as a full-blown fresh-fish dinner venue in the more formal restaurant setting inside. Madeiran specialities cohabit with pizzas and sandwiches on the food menu, *poncha* with Portuguese reds on the drinks

card. (☎291 957 697; Rua Pereira Ribeiro, Ribeira Brava; mains €7.50-18; ⊙8am-11pm)

Muralha PORTUGUESE €€

9 ✕ Map p100, D3

This crimson box and terrace above the bay is a relaxed place bedecked with traditional fishing gear. The menu is a mixed bag of grilled meat and fish, the Madeiran dishes to go for being the grilled tuna steak and *espetada*, or the roasted codfish with prawns and mussels if you're in a mainland mood. (☎291 952 592; Estrada Regional 220 1, Ribeira Brava; mains €9-16.50; ⊙11am-midnight Sun & Tue-Thu, to 2am Fri & Sat)

Understand
Fishers of Câmara de Lobos

Madeira's signature fish is the long, eel-like *espada* (scabbard fish), which is caught at night by the fisherfolk from Câmara de Lobos. These hardy souls can be seen knocking back dangerous amounts of *poncha* (an alcoholic drink based on sugar-cane spirit) in the village's many small bars before heading to the tiny Capela de Nossa Senhora da Conceição to ask for a safe night at sea. The catch is brought in early next morning and sold off to the island's markets and restaurants, after which the fisherfolk of Câmara de Lobos return to the bars to celebrate another battle with the fickle Atlantic won.

Explore

Mountains of the Interior

Madeira's mountains rise from sea level to over 1800m in just 12km, meaning this is where the island's famous 'vertical reality' takes over. The sharp basalt peaks, plunging valleys and bottomless gorges are an adventure playground in the truest sense of the words. This is also where you'll find the best of Madeira's levada hikes and long-distance trails.

The Region in a Day

To do a tour of Madeira's mountainous interior, you are going to need a car and a long day. Your first stop should be the top of **Pico do Arieiro** (p109) to catch the sunrise and enjoy the amazing views. Head back down then turn left at Poiso to Ribeiro Frio for a coffee and to watch the fishy fun at the **trout farm** (p110).

You'll have to head back down to Monte to find the road to **Curral das Freiras** (p106). Having admired the village's heart-stopping location, head to **Vale das Freiras** (p111) to lunch on local chestnut specialities. Mid-afternoon you'll have to backtrack once again to Santo António to pick up the road to Ribeira Brava and the central valley. The highest point in the valley is **Encumeada** (p109), the starting point for several long-distance trails.

From Encumeada head upwards onto the **Paúl da Serra** (p111), an eerie plateau not usually frequented by tourists. From here you can be back in Funchal for dinner in under an hour.

👁 Top Experiences

Curral das Freiras (p106)

❤ Best of the Mountains of the Interior

Walks

Pico do Arieiro to Pico Ruivo (p118)

Boca da Corrida to Encumeada (p120)

Villages

Serra de Água (p133)

Madalena do Mar (p133)

Ribeiro Frio (p133)

For Kids

Ribeiro Frio Trout Farm (p110)

Getting There

🚌 **Bus** The following buses serve the mountains from Funchal: Curral das Freiras, Horários do Funchal bus 81; Ribeiro Frio, Horários do Funchal bus 56; Encumeada, Rodoeste buses 6 and 139.

Top Experiences
Curral das Freiras

One of the most popular trips from Funchal, a day in Curral das Freiras (Nun's Valley) is that typical Madeiran combination of awe-inspiring mountain scenery, an easy-going walk, local specialities and welcoming locals. A short steep bus ride from the bustle of Funchal's seafront, this village at the bottom of a huge cauldron of rock is known for its chestnuts and a cherry liquor called *ginja,* drunk across the island from shot glasses made of dark chocolate.

⊙ Map p108, C3

www.jf-curraldasfreiras.pt

Curral das Freiras

Don't Miss

Hike from Eira do Serrado

A scenic way to approach Curral das Freiras is to take the bus to the lookout point at Eira do Serrado, 1094m above sea level and hike down from there. Enjoy the truly astounding views down to the valley floor, around 700m below, before taking the path from behind the hotel and souvenir stalls; a popular hike, the 4.5km route (around two hours) is downhill until the very last section along the road, mostly on rounded steps. Along the way high outcrops of volcanic rock make excellent picnic halts, and interesting flora such as eucalyptus trees and camphor plants scent the air.

Chestnuts

What better way to end the hike from Eira do Serrado than with some local tucker in one of Curral das Freiras' feeding spots? The local chestnuts are harvested between October and January, but are available all year round as an ingredient in soup, bread, biscuits, cakes, liquors and sweets. The village even holds a chestnut festival (Festa da Castanha) in early November and 'exports' its products to the tourist hotspots of Funchal.

Village & Surroundings

Chestnuts digesting, your next stop should be the pretty Igreja de Nossa Senhora do Livramento, interesting for its cliff-edge position just off the main road. Around Curral das Freiras are remote settlements where locals grow vegetables in ever steepening gradients the further up the valley you progress. If the hike from Eira do Serrado whetted your appetite, a much more demanding trail heads straight up the side of a mountain from north of the village, linking in with the Encumeada–Boca da Corrida trail.

☑ Top Tips

▶ It's a good idea to tackle the hike from Eira do Serrado downhill, though some do make the climb from Curral das Freiras.

▶ The path between Eira do Serrado and Curral das Freiras is safe, but care should be taken after heavy rain.

▶ Morning buses stop in Eira do Serrado, but later services miss it out.

▶ Last buses from Curral das Freiras leave late in the evening, so there's no chance of getting stranded.

✗ Take a Break

Sabores do Curral (p111) is a superb addition to the village's dining scene, lending things a slightly more gourmet feel. Otherwise Vale das Freiras (p111) has a menu of traditional chestnut-based dishes.

ER103

Ribeiro Frio

Quiemadas
Forest Park

7

5

Balcões ⊙2

Poiso

6

Ribeiro Frio
Trout Farm

Pico Ruivo
(1862m)

Pico das
Torres
(1853m)

Pico do Arieiro ⊙1

5 km
2.5 miles

0
0

Ⓝ

E

D

ER107

Curral das
Freiras ⊙

C

For reviews see
⊙ Top Experiences   p106
⊙ Experiences   p109
☒ Eating   p111

Boca da Encumeada

3 ⊙

Central Valley

ER104

Bica da
Cana 4 ⊙

ER110

Paúl da
Serra

Serra de Água

VE4

Central Valley

B

A

1

2

3

4

Ribeiro Frio Trout Farm (p110)

Experiences

Pico do Arieiro   MOUNTAIN

1 ⊙ Map p108, D3

You can drive to the top of Pico do
Arieiro, Madeira's third-highest
mountain. At the top you'll find a cafe,
a Portuguese Air Force radar station
and stupendous views. Try to get up
here for the sunrise, though you'll not
enjoy the spectacle alone.

Balcões   VIEWPOINT

2 ⊙ Map p108, E3

A 1.5km easy and well-signposted climb
out of Ribeiro Frio brings you to one of
the most spectacular viewing points on

the whole of Madeira, the aptly named
Balcões – the Balconies. From here
you get a bird's eye view of the island's
highest peaks, the huge cauldron of
rock below them and even out across
the Atlantic to the island of Porto Santo.
A snack bar hangs off the cliff edge
halfway along the path. (Ribeiro Frio)

Boca da Encumeada   MOUNTAIN PASS

3 ⊙ Map p108, B2

The Encumeada Pass sits between
the two deep-cleft valleys that almost
slice Madeira in two. From this point
1083m up, you can see both the north
and south coastlines. It's also the
starting point for several hikes and
long-distance trails. A tunnel under

Encumeada means 99% of traffic now bypasses the pass. (ER105, Encumeada)

Bica da Cana
VIEWPOINT

4 👁 Map p108, A2

Sitting above the central valley at the eastern end of the Paúl da Serra plateau, Bica da Cana serves as a picnic spot for cross-island travellers and offers wide-screen of Madeira's highest peaks across the valley. It's also known for its wind farm – a controversial addition to this highly visible location. (ER110)

Ribeiro Frio Trout Farm
FARM

5 👁 Map p108, E3

Apart from being the launch pad for some great mountain walks, Ribeiro Frio's other attraction is what must be the world's most visited trout farm. Hundreds of trout chase each other round huge tanks fed with icy cold levada water, the whole place a fishy, multilevel symphony of moving water. Don't feed the fish whatever you do – it's strictly forbidden. (Ribeiro Frio; admission free; ⊙24hr)

Understand
Madeira's Tricky Transport

As you ease your hire car through one of Madeira's modern tunnels, spare a thought for those who came before you. Until the 20th century most of the island didn't have roads. The only way to get around was on foot, or by sleds pulled by oxen. Monte's toboggans are the only remnant of this mode of transport. In the 18th and 19th centuries, Funchal's wealthy were carried around in sedan chairs.

Metalled roads were built as more cars appeared in Funchal, but what roads they are! The ability to perform a hill start is essential in these parts, as Funchal's heroic bus drivers demonstrate without a flinch of rollback.

Roads may have invaded most of the island, but there are still places accessible only by cable car. The best known *teleféricos* run between the Zona Velha, Monte and the botanical gardens, but there are several others around the coast. They often give access to farmland or beaches.

Until 1964 the only way to reach Madeira was by ship or seaplane. Santa Catarina Airport was built that year, but with a very short runway and mountains on three sides, it quickly gained a reputation as one of the world's trickiest landing strips. In 2002 the runway was lengthened from 1600m to 2780m by building out on stilts, thus creating one of the most remarkable airports in the world.

Of equal economic importance is the Via Rápida, the motorway linking Machico with Ribeira Brava. Since its construction a decade ago this bucking, weaving freeway has cut down journey times immensely and is set to be extended to Calheta in coming years.

Eating

Sabores do Curral   MADEIRAN €€

The 'Flavours of Curral' is a welcome addition to the dining scene in this tourist hotspot (see ◎ Map p108, C3). After admiring one of the most gob-smacking, cliff-edge views you'll ever experience from any restaurant, choose from the simple but well-executed menu of traditional Madeiran meat and fish dishes, with a snifter of local *ginja* (cherry liqueur) to start. (Caminho da Igreja 1, Curral das Freiras; mains €8-15; ⊙ 9am-7pm Tue-Sun)

Casa de Abrigo do Poiso   PORTUGUESE, MADEIRAN €€

6 ✘ Map p108, E3

At the turn off on the ER 103 for Pico do Arieiro, this rustic mountain refuge, easily reachable from Funchal by car, plates up Portuguese and Madeiran favourites in a welcoming, slightly old-fashioned dining room. It's just the place to reheat after a hike in the hills with a few shots of *poncha* and a bowl of hearty, warming tomato soup. (www.casaabrigopoiso.ondebiz.com; ER 103, Poiso, Camacha; mains €8-15; ⊙8.30pm-midnight Mon, 8.30am-midnight Tue-Thu & Sun, 8.30pm-2am Fri & Sat)

Restaurante Ribeiro Frio   MADEIRAN €€

7 ✘ Map p108, E3

This cosy pre- or post-levada-hike refuge is good for a full blown, calorie-replacing meal or coffee and cakes while you wait for the bus back to Funchal. With the trout farm almost opposite, it's no surprise that the rare freshwater fish dominates the menu. The wood-rich interior is warmed by cast-iron stoves, a welcome sight after a day on a damp levada. (Ribeiro Frio; mains €6.50-14.50; ⊙9am-7pm)

Vale das Freiras   MADEIRAN €€

Curral das Freiras (see ◎ Map p108, C3) is known for its chestnuts and this restaurant-cafe specialises in all sorts of dishes made from them. Chestnut soup, liquors, cakes, bread or just plain roasted chestnuts are the highlights of the menu, though there are other Madeiran staples, too. There's a complimentary chestnut liquor for everyone and an adjoining shop selling more...yes, you guessed it, chestnuts. (Caminho de Padaria 2, Curral das Freiras; mains €5-15; ⊙8am-10pm)

◯ Local Life
Paúl da Serra

Overlooked by most tourists, the lonely **Paúl da Serra** (Map p108, A2) is a high flat plateau of treeless moorland inhabited by Madeira's only cows. It was once suggested that Madeira's airport be moved up here – until someone counted how many days a year these uplands are smothered in fog.

Top Experiences
Porto Santo

Getting There

⚓ Porto Santo Line runs a daily ferry in both directions. (One-way on Fridays, except August).

✈ Aero VIP operates four services daily from Madeira (around €175, 25 minutes return)

You may hear or read the word 'archipelago' in relation to Madeira – that's because the main island is not alone. The Desertas and Selvagens islands are uninhabited, but 40km to the northeast, Madeira's sister island, Porto Santo, has a population of around 5500. Measuring just 14km by 8km, Porto Santo is a very different place to Madeira – arid, low-slung and boasting one of Europe's finest golden-sand beaches – the main reason to make the journey here.

Views from the clubhouse at Porto Santo Golfe (p114)

Don't Miss

Staying the Night

Porto Santo is touted as a day cruise from Funchal, the small ferry leaving in the morning and returning in the evening. This suits visitors with little time on their hands, but to really savour this remote outpost of the Portuguese world, consider an overnight stay. This allows you to enjoy a day on the beach and another exploring the island by bicycle or scooter. There are plenty of hotels around Vila Baleira, some offering great deals outside the summer months. The town also boasts the archipelago's biggest campsite (there are only two!), but you'll need to bring a tent.

Vila Baleira

The only settlement of any size is sleepy Vila Baleira, where you'll find the **turismo** (tourist office; ☎291 985 244; Avenida Dr Manuel Gregório Pestana Junior; ⏰9am-5.30pm Mon-Fri, 10am-12.30pm Sat) and all the island's services. It's one of the archipelago's oldest towns, founded in 1419 by the first governor Bartolomeu Perestrelo. Pretty, whitewashed Largo do Pelhourinho has a beautiful old church and lots of cafe tables.

The Beach

Extending around 7.5km from the ferry port to the island's southernmost point, Ponta da Calheta, Porto Santo's beach is nothing short of spectacular; it is regularly voted one of the top 10 stretches of sand in Europe (though it's not actually in Europe). The large grains are tiny fragments of coral, the remains of reefs dating back 20 million years. Gently shelving into the cooling Atlantic and backed by Porto Santo's long-since-extinct volcano cones, this is a place you'll want to linger until the ferry departs. In summer the beach attracts Portuguese families escaping the heat of the mainland; in winter you can have it to yourself.

Capital: Vila Baleira

www.porto-santo.com

☑ Top Tips

▶ The ferry to Porto Santo is often cancelled due to bad weather – no refunds are offered, but you can rebook.

▶ The island is best visited in the summer months when things are livelier.

▶ Car and scooter hire is available (on the seafront in Vila Baleira), so there's no need to bring your own hire car.

✕ Take a Break

Pé na Água (Sítio das Pedras Pretas, Vila Baleia; ⏰11am-11pm) is a beach restaurant and bar to the west of Vila Baleira serving seafood, steaks and pastas. **Baiana** (Largo do Pelhourinho, Vila Baleia; ⏰9am-1am), on the square in Vila Baleira, is a convenient, popular and informal restaurant where the large portions of seafood come particularly recommended.

Columbus House

The only bona fide 'sight' is the **Casa Museu Colombo** (www.museucolombo-portosanto.com; Travessa da Sacristia 2/4, Vila Baleira; admission €2; ⏱10am-noon & 2-5.30pm Tue-Sat, 10am-1pm Sun Oct-Jun, to 7pm Tue-Sat Jul-Sep), just off Largo do Pelhourinho. It's claimed Christopher Columbus lived here. The museum contains exhibitions on the colonisation of the New World and Columbus' voyages, but as there's no real evidence Columbus actually lived in this particular house, the information on the famous explorer is a bit vague and based more on popular myth than historical fact.

Volcanic Peaks

Porto Santo is a much older island than Madeira (by around 13 million years) and the volcanoes that pushed through the Atlantic's surface have been worn down by rain and wind into odd-shaped peaks. The highest of these is **Pico do Facho** (516m), northeast of Vila Baleira, where fires were once lit to warn Madeira of impending pirate attack. Directly north of the 'capital' is **Pico Castelo** (437m) and in the far southwest is **Pico de Ana Ferreira** (283m), both of which can be climbed for magnificent Macaronesian views.

The Rest of the Island

If you hire a bike, scooter or car, the island can be seen in a couple of hours. Porto Santo's airport is an odd spectacle, extending almost the entire width of the island! **Porto Santo Golfe** (📞291 983 778; www.portosantogolfe.com; Sítio das Marinhas; 9 holes €40, 18 holes €72) is arguably the archipelago's best course. Designed by Seve Ballesteros, its 18 holes regularly make it into the world's top 100 golf courses. The **Portela viewpoint** provides views of the whole island and is a popular 2½-hour hike from Vila Baleira; ask at the tourist office for details.

Understand

Columbus on Porto Santo

Local myth paints a romantic picture – a 27-year-old Colombus, strolling Porto Santo's jaw-droppingly beautiful beach, picking up exotic seeds washed up by the Atlantic, looking to the horizon and wondering what might lie beyond…

But how did the man who went on to discover America come to be on this micro-island in the Atlantic? Commissioned to buy sugar on Madeira by a Lisbon merchant house, Colombus arrived in Funchal in 1478. He probably knew Porto Santo's governor, Bartolomeu Perestrelo II, son of the island's first governor, from their early days in Genoa. Colombus married his daughter, Dona Felipa Moniz, that same year and moved to Madeira's lesser sibling. But in 1479 tragedy struck when Felipa and their new-born son died, leaving Colombus alone to wander and wonder. He left soon after and the rest, as they say in these parts, is *história*.

Pico de Facho (516m)

Pico Castelo (437m)

Ferry Port

Airport

VILA BALEIRA

Beach

Porto Santo Golfe

Pico de Ana Ferreira (283m)

Ilhéu de Baixo

ATLANTIC OCEAN

2 km
1 mile
0
0

The Best of
Madeira

Madeira's Best Walks

Pico do Arieiro to Pico Ruivo 118

Boca da Corrida to Encumeada . . . 120

Ponta de São Lourenço 122

Madeira's Best...

Eating 124

Drinking & Nightlife 126

Shopping. 127

Museums & Galleries 128

Tours 129

For Kids 130

Festivals & Events 131

Beaches & Sea Swimming 132

Villages 133

For Free 134

Wine Tasting 135

Parks & Gardens. 136

Traditional toboggan drivers' straw hats, Monte (p68)
MERTEN SNIJDERS/GETTY IMAGES ©

Best Walks
Pico do Arieiro to Pico Ruivo

🏃 The Walk

Arguably the best walk on Madeira, this occasionally challenging mountain hike links the third-highest peak, Pico do Arieiro, with the highest, Pico Ruivo, via the second-highest, Pico das Torres. Above the clouds, the views are astounding, but come prepared – sturdy footwear, warm clothes, a torch, water and food are essentials. The walk can be done independently, but with rockfalls an issue, a guide is recommended. An organised hike also solves the problem of how to get to Pico do Arieiro and from Achada do Teixeira, the nearest to Pico Ruivo vehicles can reach.

Start Pico do Arieiro

Finish Pico Ruivo

Length 8.6km; four hours

🍴 Take a Break

The snack bar at Pico do Arieiro sells hot-dogs, sandwiches and drinks. The refuge at Pico Ruivo does drinks but little food. Bring a picnic.

HOLGER LEUE/GETTY IMAGES ©

Hikers near Pico Ruivo summit

❶ Pico do Arieiro

Early mornings are busy at the top of Madeira's third-highest mountain (1818m). Some are having breakfast in the cafe with the best view from any Madeiran eatery, others are making adjustments to kit or just taking snaps of the surrounding mountainscape. But PR1, the trail to Pico Ruivo, awaits.

❷ Ninho da Manta

Around 20 minutes into the hike and the first stop for most is Ninho da Manta or Buzzard's Nest, a *miradouro* (viewpoint) with astounding views down to the Penha D'Aguía (the Eagle's Rock), a huge coastal mountain that locals claim looks like the head of an eagle. From up here it doesn't.

❸ Túnel do Pico do Gato

After around 45 minutes that torch you brought comes in handy as you enter the almost complete darkness of the first tunnel on the route. Pico do Gato – Cat's Peak – refers to the mountain you see as you emerge back into the sun/fog.

④ Fork in the Road

One hour in and the path splits. To the left is the easier route through several tunnels. To the right is a longer, harder path. We are going right.

⑤ Pico das Torres

After a long climb a split in the rock at around the one-hour-40-minute mark announces you have arrived at Pico das Torres (1853m), Madeira's second-highest mountain. At last you can see your destination, the refuge and Pico Ruivo seemingly just across the way, but still two hours distant.

⑥ Take the Tunnel

At around the 2½-hour mark, there's another split in the path, but this time the decision about which way to go has been taken for you. A barrier has been erected to prevent hikers accessing the old path that was obliterated a few years

ago by a rock fall. Take the tunnel to access the new trail.

⑦ Pico Ruivo

By the three-hours-40-minute mark you should have reached the mountain refuge just below Pico Ruivo. Many call it a day here, but the top is only half a kilometre away and it's worth it for the stupendous views, the best Madeira can offer – and that's saying something.

Best Walks
Boca da Corrida to Encumeada

🏃 The Walk

Easily accessible by bus from Funchal, this is a dramatic mountain walk through the mountainscape of Madeira but without the climbs usually involved. The path, known as the Caminha Real da Encumeada (Encumeada Royal Path; PR12), was one of the main horse and foot routes across the island before roads were built. The clearly marked and well-maintained route skirts the foot of some of Madeira's highest peaks, taking you well above the tree line. This lack of shade can be a problem when the sun is out, so take sun cream. This route should not be tackled in high winds or when heavy rain is forecast.

Start Boca da Corrida

Finish Encumeada

Length 12.5km; four hours

🍴 Take a Break

Taking a picnic along is the only way to go. There are no places to eat until you reach Encumeada.

❶ Corrida

Rodoeste bus 96 leaves Funchal twice in the morning for Corrida. Just the ride, a seemingly almost vertical climb from Câmara de Lobos, is an invigorating start to the day. Buses deposit hikers (you won't be alone) at a lonely terminus from where it's a stiff climb up an asphalt road to the start of the hike.

❷ Boca da Corrida

It takes a good half an hour to reach Boca da Corrida, the start of the walk. Here you'll find a tiny chapel and views across the mammoth valley at the top of which is the village of Curral das Freiras. Most loiter a while here before setting out onto marked trail PR12.

❸ Boca de Cerro

By the time you reach the Boca de Cerro (1¼ hours), it's probably time for lunch and this is a good spot to de-bag supplies. An alternative walk from here is to take the badly signposted trail down to Curral das Freiras, though

Mountains and valleys around Encumeada Pass

this extremely steep, exposed route is not for the faint-hearted.

❹ Pico Grande Escarpment

After Boca de Cerro the path narrows, but is still very easy to pick out. At the 90-minute mark you begin to edge your way around the base of the escarpment of Pico Grande, one of the island's highest mountains. In March the gorse here is in full bloom, making the hillsides look as though they are ablaze.

❺ Ribeira do Poço Valley

From Pico Grande the path begins its descent towards Encumeada. After around 2½ hours you enter the valley of the Ribeira do Poço, a lush and verdant stretch that contrasts markedly with the bare rock the path has crossed for most of the way. You traverse the river via a stone bridge.

❻ Encumeada

The path weaves its way down to the valley until it becomes a track.

This leads to the main road, which crosses the Encumeada Pass. From here you can walk down to the Residencial Encumeada for a coffee and catch the bus back to Funchal (Rodoeste buses 6 and 139). Check the timetables before you leave Funchal.

Best Walks
Ponta de São Lourenço

🏃 The Walk

This there-and-back coastal hike takes hikers to the far eastern end of Madeira, the Ponta de São Lourenço peninsula. The trail along the island's snaking, undulating tail is a very different beast to the famous levada walks, with lots of ups and downs and no shade when the sun is out as there are virtually no trees. That lack of vegetation means nothing gets in the way of the Atlantic panoramas, which at some points will leave you breathless. Those views bring out the crowds in good weather, so sadly this isn't one for solitude seekers.

Start Baía D'Abra; SAM bus 113

Finish Baía D'Abra; SAM bus 113

Length 8km; four hours

🍴 Take a Break

There are plenty of ideal spots along the way for a picnic with a view and taking along your own supplies is definitely the best way to go.

CHRISTIAN GOUP/GETTY IMAGES ©

Sea cliffs, Ponta de São Lourenço

❶ Baía D'Abra

Buses and taxis leave hikers at the Baía D'Abra car park, where you'll find a route map (numbered PR8) but little else. With the number of hikers around, you'd expect to find souvenir stalls and refreshments but these are conspicuous by their absence!

❷ Take a Dip

Around 15 to 20 minutes into the hike you reach a crossroads in the trail. Take a right and follow the rough path down to a very secluded beach. In the morning you'll have this and the views of the Desertas to yourself.

❸ Seahorse Rocks

Head up from the beach and keep going straight on. This dead end has camera-friendly views of the seahorse rocks, toweringly stranded chunks of volcanic rock that the seething Atlantic has separated from the mothership, the reds and greys of the rocks contrasting photogenically with the white surf.

❹ Left or Right?

An information board giving details of the protected area you are passing through stands at the beginning/end of the loop around the end of the accessible part of the peninsula. It doesn't matter which way you go, as you'll end up back here. We're going left.

❺ Cais do Sardinha

Built by Manuel Bettencourt Sardinha in 1905 as a holiday home, this pretty, tropical oasis of a house was sold to the regional government by his granddaughter in 1996 and now serves as a reception centre for the protected area. Shaded by palm trees, the picnic tables here provide the perfect lunch spot.

❻ Morro do Furado

Behind the Cais do Sardinha rises the Morro do Furado, a huge hillside marking the end of the peninsula's accessible section. It's a bit of a slog to the top on crumbly and slippery ground, but the Atlantic panoramas from the top are magnificent. The island of Porto Santo is clearly visible to the north on clear days.

❼ Quay & Beach

Looping back, just past the birdwatching post, a short path runs down to a small quay and beach, a secluded spot even when the trail is busy. Swimming and diving are permitted. From here retrace your steps back to Baía D'Abra.

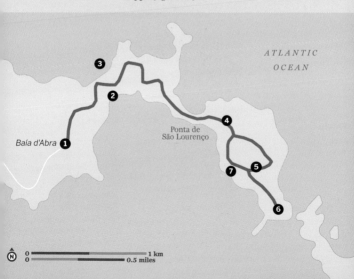

Best
Eating

Eating is one of the joys of visiting Madeira and most will admit the island's fare is tastebud-friendly. Variety was once an issue but innovative chefs are introducing a touch of imagination in line with mainland trends. Restaurants are of a good standard everywhere; for quick bites, countless owner-run cafes are cheap as chips.

Seafood

Seafood is the big draw, though some restaurants do feature salmon, fruits de mer, prawns and other creatures not from Madeira's waters. Limpets are about the only shellfish native to Madeira.

Espada vs Espetada

The *espada* (scabbard fish) is the eel-like monster that will catch your eye at the Mercado dos Lavradores. Caught at night deep in the Atlantic, this spiky-toothed, jelly-eyed beast tastes better than it looks. You'll only find it on Madeira and some expensive restaurants in Lisbon. *Espetada* is chunks of beef, smothered in garlic-and-laurel-leaf-infused butter, skewered on a laurel wand and grilled over acacia embers. Many confuse the two!

Fancy Fruits

On a trip around the island, you'll see many odd fruits dangling. These are most likely the *anona* (custard apple), the pineapple banana, papaya or the *tomate inglês* (tamarillo). Madeira's own sweet miniature bananas are instantly recognisable.

Sugar & Spice

Bolo de mel (sugar syrup cake) tastes a bit like Christmas pudding and is eaten around that time. Sugarcane biscuits, eucalyptus-infused sweets and custardy Portuguese creations are also widely consumed.

Best
Seafood

Gavião Novo
One of Funchal's best seafood restaurants buried deep in the Zona Velha. (p59)

Maré Alta
Head to Machico's seafront to enjoy great grilled fish. (p86)

Best
New & Funky

Oficina
Good spot in Funchal for a lunchtime vegie burger or an evening in the company of cocktails and a DJ. (p60)

Hamburgueria do Mercado
Madeira's first gourmet burger joint in Funchal's new Armazém do Mercado complex. (p60)

Man cooking *espetada* (skewered beef)

Boho Bistrô
Petite bistro in a busy location in downtown Funchal. (p40)

Best Traditional Madeiran

O Celeiro
A typical Madeiran tavern serving high-quality local dishes in Funchal. (p40)

Venda da Donna Maria
Food like granny used to make in an imaginative Zona Velha dining space. (p61)

Cantinho da Serra
Honestly made traditional food in a rural location near the north-coast village of Santana. (p76)

Best Fine Dining

La Perla
Dine on gourmet fare in an elegant *quinta* (mansion) setting in Caniço. (p86)

Il Gallo d'Oro
One of Madeira's best dining options with the Michelin star to prove it. (p40)

Best
Drinking
& Nightlife

Until a few years ago nightlife on Madeira was limited to dinner and a show at the casino, one nightclub and possibly an overdose of sickly *poncha*. How times have changed, with numerous new bars now spilling out onto the streets and DJs disc-spinning until the early weekend hours, though 99% of the fun is still in Funchal.

Madeiran Drinks

Madeira has several beverages you might not experience anywhere else. *Poncha* is a local favourite – proper *poncha* (pictured) should be made fresh and should only contain *aguardente de cana* (sugar-cane alcohol), sugar, honey and lemon. Despite what some tour guides might say, Madeirans do *not* drink it to cure a cold! Swift inebriation can be achieved with neat *aguardente,* but *ginja* – a sweet cherry liquor from Curral das Freiras – drunk from a chocolate cup is a much more pleasant experience. Produced in Funchal city centre, Corral is the island's favourite beer.

Best Drinking

Barreirinha Cafe
Balmy nights of caipirinhas as the Atlantic crashes onto the rocks below. (p62)

Cafe do Museu
Late drinking spot on pretty Praça do Município. (p43)

Prince Albert Pub
Funchal's longest-established British pub. (p42)

Santa Maria Gin Bar
Great new minimalist bar with an obsession for mother's ruin. (p62)

Best Nightlife

Arsenio's
Renowned Funchal nightspot for that favoured combination of grilled meat, wine and fado music. (p64)

Vespas
Cut some shapes at Madeira's grooviest temple to the god of night. (p42)

Casino da Madeira
Show, dinner and a quick spin of roulette. (p44)

Cafe do Teatro
DJs bring weekend nights to life at the old theatre cafe. (p42)

Copacabana
Glamorous hang-out where you can fritter away your winnings from the casino next door. (p42)

Best
Shopping

There have been some funky moves afoot in the Madeiran shopping experience in recent years. Tired of the same old made-in-China banana fridge magnets and fake Ronaldo football shirts, young entrepreneurs have been jazzing up the market, producing cool mementos with a younger, hipper vibe. Otherwise look for real traditional handmade items in Funchal's more upmarket souvenir emporia.

DANITA DELIMONT/GETTY IMAGES ©

Mementos Made in Madeira

In the last decade there's been real upsurge in pride for real Madeiran-made goods and souvenirs. The 'Made in Madeira' sticker can now be seen on many items in shops, but just what does the island produce in the way of souvenirs? The obvious duo are wine and embroidery, the production of which is strictly regulated by IVBAM (Instituto do Vinho, do Bordado e do Artesanato da Madeira). Cakes and sweets such as *bolo de mel, poncha,* jewellery, Caniçal whale-bone carvings, Camacha wicker and sugar-cane biscuits are other genuine made-in-Madeira items.

Armazém do Mercado
This new pop-up space for local producers and artisans also holds an organic market. (p64)

Patrício & Gouveia
Funchal's classiest souvenir emporium selling the island's best traditional wares. (p64)

Casa do Turista
Museum-like souvenir shop specialising exclusively in the best items from Madeira and Portugal. (p45)

Bordal
The place to buy traditional Madeiran embroidery and watch this cottage industry in action. (p67)

O Relogio
Wicker wonders come in all shapes and sizes at this emporium above the weaving workshop. (p82)

Mercado dos Lavradores
Funchal's famous market, bursting with colourful produce from the 'garden of the Atlantic'. (p52)

Livraria Esperança
Huge second-hand and new bookstore; in fact, it's Portugal's biggest. (p45)

Saudade Madeira
Unique items from tens of tiny producers across the island, plus a great cafe and workshops. (p46)

Madeira Lovers
New, funky souvenir company, the antidote to Madeira's often cheap and tired-looking mementos. (p66)

Best Museums & Galleries

Madeira's excellent museums examine almost every aspect of island life past and present often in an interactive, hands-on way. Inexpensive, well-curated and open when you want them to be, these repositories of the island's past are some of the non-outdoor highlights of time spent on Madeira. Visit them all and you'll be an expert on what made and makes Madeira tick.

Quinta das Cruzes
See how the other (richer) half lived in the antique Funchal of yesteryear. (p24)

Museu da Baleia
In Caniçal, this is possibly the greatest whale-themed museum in the world. (p85)

Museu Etnográfico da Madeira A must for anyone with more than a passing interest in traditional life on the island; Ribeira Brava. (p101)

Museu CR7 Unique Funchal museum dedicated to the most famous Madeiran of all time, footballer Cristiano Ronaldo. (p36)

Casa Museu Frederico de Freitas This Funchal mansion is a paradise for anyone who's ever collected anything. (p36)

Museu de Arte Sacra
Madeira's premier art collection with pieces from across the island. (p26)

Museu Photographia Vicentes Discover Madeira's past through the camera lens. (p36)

Casa da Luz – Museu de Electricidade
Whoever thought a museum dedicated to electricity generation could be this interesting? (p57)

☑ Top Tips

▶ Most Madeiran museums close at least one day a week, normally Sunday or Monday.

▶ Surprisingly Madeira has no tourist card giving discounts on entry, though most museums charge very little to get in anyway, around €3.

▶ Some, though definitely not all, of the island's museums have a lunch break, so check the opening times before you set out.

Best
Tours

Tukxi (☎291 207 083; www.tukxi.pt; Rua dos Aranhas 53; tours per tuk tuk from €30) Tukxi uses a fleet of 10 electric Ape Calessinos to zip visitors around the city on a variety of tours led by very knowledgeable driver-guides. An innovative and eco-friendly way to see Funchal.

City Bubble Tours

(☎291 782 855; www.city bubbles.pt; Estrada Monumental, Edifício Atlântida; 1hr €26, 4hr €50, day €60; ⏰10am-8pm) These electric, two-seater Renault Twizys have become a popular, fun and eco-friendly way of whizzing round Madeira. Preset tours are GPS-guided and there are charging points at strategic locations around the island.

Rota dos Cetáceos

(☎291 280 600; www.rota-dos-cetaceos.pt; Marinia Shopping, Avenida Arriaga 75; adult/child €48/33; ⏰8.45am, 12.30pm & 4pm Jul-Sep, 9am & 1.30pm Oct-Jun) Four-hour whale- and dolphin-watching tours in the company of marine biologists. If you don't see what you came to see, the company will take you again free of charge.

Madeira Explorers

(☎291 763 701; www. madeira-levada-walks.com; shop 23, 1st fl, Monumental Lido; per half/full day €27/37) Professional outfit running levada hikes and other walks across the island. Hotel pick-up and drop-off included in the price.

Ventura (Map p34; ☎963 691 995; www.venturadomar. com; Funchal Marina) This company operates yacht tours to the uninhabited Desertas and Selvagens islands as well as birdwatching trips, dolphin- and whale-spotting tours and canyoning outings into the mountainous interior.

MERTEN SNIJDERS/GETTY IMAGES ©

History Tellers

(☎291 705 060; www. historytellers.pt; Armazém do Mercado, Rua Latino Coelho 39; tour €5; ⏰10am-8pm Mon-Sat, to 6pm Sun) Informative walking tours of Funchal given by clued-up student volunteers. All proceeds go into scholarships and the student union at the University of Madeira.

Best
For Kids

Despite Madeira's now slightly outdated image as a destination for old folk, it's actually one of the most enjoyable places in 'Europe' to bring the kids, especially during the northern hemisphere winter, and more and more parents are doing so. Which kid wouldn't enjoy Madeira's black-sand beaches, countless playgrounds, sunny weather and cafes stacked with tons of sweet stuff?

Loving Locals

But it's really the Madeirans themselves who make this such a child-friendly place to holiday – little 'uns are more than welcome absolutely everywhere and made a fuss of wherever they go. Bus drivers will rarely take a fare for a child and in restaurants you can be sure of that little bit of extra food should you have a child with you.

Best Museums

Museu da Baleia 3D films, giant suspended whale models and a simulated submarine journey! (p85)

Casa da Luz – Museu de Electricidade Electrifying hands-on experiments. (p57)

Centro Ciência Viva Learning by stealth at this interactive centre focusing on Madeira's Unesco-listed laurisilva forests. (p75)

Museu CR7 An absolute must for any football fan. (p36; pictured above)

Museu do Brinquedo Toys of yesteryear. (p58)

Best Animal Encounters

Aquário da Madeira Go nose to nose with a shark without losing body parts. (p75)

Ribeiro Frio Trout Farm Two things that kids love – flowing water and living creatures – come together here. (p110)

Best Excitement

Grutas e Centro do Vulcanismo Descend into the molten centre of the earth Jules Verne style. (p75)

Aeroporto da Madeira Plane spotting as you watch pilots perform tricky landing manoeuvres. (p85)

Parque Temático da Madeira Tons of fun rowing boats, clambering around the playground and getting lost in the maze. (p75)

Monte Toboggans Use your air steering wheel as you enjoy a toboggan ride down from Monte. (p69)

Best
Festivals & Events

Carnaval
(Avenidas Sá Carneiro & do Mar; ⏰40 days before Easter) The calendar's biggest party hits Funchal in late winter when the island is busiest. One of the world's best carnivals, the main attraction is the 9pm two-hour-long procession along Funchal's seafront, a spectacle you won't forget, complete with samba drums, hundreds of dancing girls, Brazilian rhythms and outrageous floats, all vividly illuminated against the ink-black Atlantic night.

Funchal Marathon
(www.funchalmarathon.com; ⏰early Mar) Marathon, half marathon and fun runs that mostly avoid Funchal's hills.

Festa da Flor
(⏰late Apr; pictured above) Carnaval 'take two' is an incredibly colourful celebration of Madeira's diverse plantlife with floats weighed down in blossoms and a parade passing through Funchal's city centre to a samba beat.

Festival do Atlântico
(www.festivalatlantico. com; ⏰10.30pm every Sat in Jun) Madeira has a tradition of lighting the blue touch paper – the Atlantic's greatest pyromaniacs have held the world record for the biggest display a couple of times. This Funchal festival celebrates the art of the pyrotechnician over four Saturday nights in June.

Festa de Nossa Senhora do Monte
(Monte; ⏰15 Aug) Food, flowers and faith combine to celebrate the island's patron saint, the Lady of Monte. Held in Monte around the Igreja da Nossa Senhora.

HOLGER LEUE/GETTY IMAGES ©

Noite do Mercado
(⏰evening 23 Dec) Locals gather at the Mercado dos Lavradores and its surrounding streets to eat, drink and wish each other a merry Christmas until the small hours.

Fim do Ano (⏰31 Dec) The second biggest bash of the year (after Carnaval) with a gargantuan fireworks display that uses the entire city of Funchal as a pyrotechnical amphitheatre.

Best
Beaches &
Sea Swimming

Praia Formosa/ do Arieiro (Rua da Praia Formosa) Anyone who claims Madeira has no beaches should hop on bus 1 or 43 to the boulders and browny-black sand of this wild strand in Funchal's western suburbs. Cafe-bars, a car park and other facilities are all here and the salt-white Atlantic surf crashing onto dark volcanic sand is a sight you'll long remember.

Praia de Machico (Rua do Leiria, Machico; pictured above) Gently sloping sun-trap beach created with golden sand shipped in from Morocco and protected by two man-made breaks. Facilities include toilets, volleyball court and showers. There are lots of places to eat nearby.

Praia da Calheta (Rua Dom Manuel I, Calheta) Two well-protected artificial beaches (created with sand from western Sahara) face each other off on Calheta's seafront, one of the sunniest places on the island. A great place to swim on hot days and there are plenty of feeding spots nearby.

Piscinas Naturais (Rua dos Emigrantes & Rua do Forte de São João Baptista, Porto Moniz; admission €1.50; ⊘9am-5.30pm) Natural pools made of volcanic rock (assisted by a dab of concrete here and there) can be found at both ends of Porto Moniz seafront. Those near the Cachalote restaurant are free and wild. Those at the other end charge admission, are a touch tamer and are better for swimming.

Praia de Garajau (Estrada do Cristo Rei, Garajau; cable car single/ return €2/2.50) At the foot of the cliff atop which stands the *Cristo Rei* statue, this stony beach was once used for dismembering and boiling up whales caught by boats off Madeira. It's since been turned into a leisure complex with a restaurant and other facilities reached by cable car or a very long and zigzagging road.

Complexo Balnear Lido Galomar (www.galoresort.com; Ponta da Oliveira, Caniço de Baixo) Take the lift down from Caniço de Baixo's Hotel Galomar to discover this secluded sun-trapping bathing area with sea access, pools and a first-rate restaurant.

Best **Villages**

Ponta do Sol
The island's sunniest spot with a rocky beach and pretty, compact centre (pictured right). Worth a stop on the way between Funchal and Calheta.

Ribeira Brava
Busy, scenic and just a short drive from Funchal, 'Wild River' is one of the nicest spots on Madeira. Leave the touristy seafront and head for the mesh of lanes behind containing old-fashioned shops and tiny cafes frequented by the locals.

Serra de Água (ER104)
Jammed into the central valley that cleaves Madeira asunder, this picturesque village of 1000 souls is slightly off the beaten track.

It's surrounded by high mountains and terraces on which locals grow produce.

Madaiena do Mar (ER101)
Wedged into the mouth of an impossibly deep creek, tiny Madalena do Mar has a long stony beach and a quiet, undisturbed atmosphere that feels a long way from Funchal.

Paúl do Mar (ER223)
Perching precariously on a ledge under high cliffs, pretty Paúl do Mar is Madeira's surfing capital and has even hosted a leg of the World Surfing Championships.

Ribeiro Frio (ER103)
'Cold River', deep in the mountains but under the tree line, is the chilly

MERTEN SNIJDERS/GETTY IMAGES ©

jumping-off point for some levada walks and has a couple of cosy eateries heated with log fires.

São Vicente (ER101/104)
This large north-coast village boasts a top Madeira attraction (Grutas e Centro do Vulcanismo) as well as an attractive square, a pretty basalt-and-whitewash church and a rocky beach lined with cafes and restaurants.

Best
For Free

MERTEN SNIJDERS/GETTY IMAGES ©

Until recently Madeira was generally perceived as a relatively upmarket destination, but oddly enough, it's also a place where your stash of euros will go a very long way. Bus fares and cafe meals are just two of the common costs where prices surprise many. There's also a lot that won't cost you a single euro cent!

No Cash Required

There are no paid beaches on the island and all facilities at the various places where there is natural or imported sand are free. Not a single church charges admission, there are no toll booths at the starting points of the levada walks and many of Madeira's amazing gardens and parks won't cost you a thing. Wine tasting is also a complimentary experience, with all the wine houses offering at least two free samples. The best things in life are often free and that is certainly true when it comes to the island's kicking events calendar. Unless you buy a VIP seat, one of Europe's greatest shows, Funchal's Carnaval, is free for anyone to watch.

Sé You don't need a ticket to get into Madeira's cathedral. (p28)

Zona Velha Wander this atmospheric neighbourhood at no cost. (p50)

Praia Formosa Leave your wallet at home as you enjoy the black volcanic sand at this wild Atlantic beach. (p132)

Casa do Turista There's no charge to admire the displays at this central Funchal souvenir emporium. (p45)

Cabo Girão They may have to actually pay some people to step out onto the glass viewing platform that hangs 580m above the waves. (p101)

Mercado dos Lavradores One of Madeira's top sights is free to visit – assuming you don't buy anything that is. (p52; pictured)

Camacha Wicker Factory It's free to get in, though most people can't resist buying something at this wicker-factory-cum-shop. (p82)

Aeroporto da Madeira Watch the Boeings and Airbuses from Europe swooping into Madeira's airport. (p85)

Jardim Panorâmico Lovely sun-trap gardens in the Hotel Zone with no admission charge. (p31)

Santana's A-frame houses You can wander in and out of Santana's traditional abodes at will. (p76)

Best
Wine Tasting

Henriques & Henriques
(www.henriquesehenriques.
pt; Avenida da Autonomia 10,
Câmara de Lobos; admission
free; ⏰9am-1pm & 2.30-
5.30pm Mon-Fri) Widely
regarded by those in
the know as the island's
best wine producer,
Henriques & Henriques
only uses grapes from its
own vineyards in Quinta
Grande and Câmara de
Lobos and finishes off
the wine in huge barrels
at its modern, specially
designed headquarters.
Visitors can try the four
types of three-year-old
wine for free.

Blandy's (www.blandys.
com; Avenida Arriaga
28, Funchal; tour €5.50;
⏰guided tours 10.30am,
2.30pm, 3.30pm &
4.30pm Mon-Fri, 11am Sat)
Housed in the Adegas
de São Francisco, the
former Franciscan
monastery, Blandy's
brings together the
British-Madeiran wine

companies that were
given special trading
rights with Britain in
the 17th century. The
best-known of Madeira's
wine experiences, the
45-minute tours here are
led by clued-up guides
and there are two free
samples at the end of
the tour.

Pereira D'Oliveira
(http://perolivinhos.pai.pt;
Rua dos Ferreiros 107,
Funchal; admission free;
⏰9am-6pm Mon-Fri,
9.30-1pm Sat) Funchal's
most easily accessible
wine experience, anyone
can enter the strongly
aromatic barrel room in
central Funchal and try
almost as much wine
as they please, usually
accompanied by a wedge
of *bolo de mel*. Bottles
of wine dating back to
the early 20th century
line the walls and the
company offers good
shipping deals on wine
you buy.

Borges (www.hmborges.
com; Rua 31 de Janeiro
83, Funchal; admission
free; ⏰9am-12.30pm &
2-5.30pm Mon-Fri) The
smallest of Funchal's
Madeira wine operations,
the diminutive, timber-
rich tasting room here
feels like the furthest
away from the tourist
crush and is the quiet-
est of the wineries. Any
two of the excellent
wines (up to 20 years
old) can be tasted free
of charge, often with a
complimentary chunk of
bolo de mel.

Best
Parks & Gardens

A true highlight of any trip to Madeira is visiting one of the island's many gardens, subtropical oases packed with flora (and occasionally fauna) that never fail to amaze with their colour, whatever the season. Gardens typically feature traditional Madeiran pebble pathways, polished smooth by generations of visitors, signs giving a plant's origin and Portuguese and Latin names, a cafe and great views. Only a couple of gardens charge admission.

DANITA DELIMONT/GETTY IMAGES ©

Perfect Habitat

Gardens often feature a mix of European, South African and South American trees, shrubs and plants, which find Madeira's year-round warmth and plentiful water the ideal habitat to sprout and blossom. In the 19th century, this fact was appreciated by British gardening fanatics who created many of the wonderful patches of green that dot Funchal. Plant-spotting books in English are widely available from Funchal bookshops and you'll certainly need one to identify some of the species that grow here.

Jardins Botânicos da Madeira

King of Madeira's parks and gardens and one of the world's best botanical gardens, set high above Funchal. (p54; pictured)

Jardins do Palheiro

One of the finest gardens on the island can be found on the outskirts of Funchal. (p57)

Quinta Vigia

The Madeiran president's very own garden, boasting subtropical plants and a squawking aviary. (p38)

Jardim Municipal

Lush and verdant tropical park right in the thick of the action in Funchal. (p38)

Jardim de Santa Luzia

Undervisited piece of city-centre greenery with a superb kids' playground. (p38)

Parque de Santa Catarina

Sloping lawns dotted with picnickers enjoying the views of the cruise port. (p38)

Quinta da Boa Vista

The best place to see Madeira's famous orchids in full bloom. (p59)

Survival Guide

Before You Go   138

When to Go 138
Book Your Stay 138

Arriving in Madeira   139

Getting Around   140

Bus 140
Car & Motorcycle 141
Taxi 141
Bicycle 142
Boat 142

Essential Information   142

Business Hours 142
Electricity 142
Emergencies 142
Money 142
Public Holidays 143
Safe Travel 143
Telephone Services 143
Toilets 144
Tourist Information 144
Travellers with Disabilities 144
Visas 144

Language   145

Survival Guide

Before You Go

When to Go

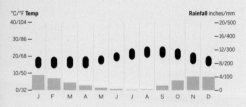

°C/°F Temp
40/104 —
30/86 —
20/68 —
10/50 —
0/32 —

Rainfall inches/mm
—20/500
—16/400
—12/300
—8/200
—4/100
—0

J F M A M J J A S O N D

➡ **Summer (Apr–Oct)**
Madeira is slightly quieter in the summer months when temperatures rise and southern Europeans come to escape the heat of the continent. Best time for swimming and beach fun but hiking can be a sweaty affair.

➡ **Winter (Oct–Mar)**
Northern Europeans fill Funchal, the temperature drops to around 18°C by day but plants from the southern hemisphere flower. Storms can hit between November and March. New Year and Carnaval (February or March) are top events.

Book Your Stay

➡ The vast majority of visitors stay in Funchal. There are options outside the city but forget these if you are relying on public transport to get around.

➡ Most of Funchal's beds are in the Hotel Zone, the area along the coast west of the city centre.

➡ Despite being packed with all of Madeira's big modern hotels, the Hotel Zone is a pleasant place.

➡ Some of the most stylish places to stay outside the Hotel Zone are quintas, hotels created in Madeira's old mansion houses.

Useful Websites

Madeira Rural (www.madeirarural.com) Villas, cottages and other accommodation in rural locations.

Lonely Planet (www.lonelyplanet.com) Author-recommendations, reviews and online booking.

Madeira Apartments
(www.madeiraapartments.com) Villas, cottages and apartments in a variety of locations.

Madeira Web
(www.madeira-web.com) All of Madeira's best hotels in one site.

Pestana Group
(www.pestana.com) Book direct with Pestana, which owns several luxury hotels on the island.

Best Budget

29 Madeira Hostel
(www.29madeirahostel.com) Funchal's newest hostel in a beautifully restored 1930s city-centre town house.

Santa Maria Hostel
(www.santamariafunchal.com) Large hostel in a former Zona Velha school with a top-notch restaurant and bar.

Pousada dos Vinháticos
(www.dorisol.com) One for walkers as it's perched high between Serra de Água and the Encumeada Pass.

Parque de Campismo do Porto Moniz
(www.portomoniz.pt) The only campsite on Madeira, located in Ribeira da Janela near Porto Moniz.

Residencial Zarco (www.residencialzarco.com) No prizes for decor but the location on Funchal's city-centre seafront is unbeatable.

Best Midrange

Quinta do Monte (www.quintadomontemadeira.com) Traditional *quinta* hotel in Monte, complete with tropical gardens.

Quinta Splendida
(www.quintasplendida.com) Well-appointed hotel in Caniço with rooms spread throughout a set of stunning Madeiran gardens.

Calheta Beach Hotel
(www.calheta-beach.com) Excellent hotel located by the artificial beach on Calheta seafront.

Madeira Panorâmico Hotel (www.madeira-panoramico.com) Vista-rich hotel set high above the Atlantic in São Martinho.

O Colmo (www.hotelocolmo-santana.com) Inexpensive but good-quality hotel on the main street in Santana.

Best Top End

Cliff Bay (www.portobay.com) A luxurious, award-winning hotel in Funchal's Hotel Zone.

Estalgem Ponta do Sol (www.pontadosol.com) Stylish, minimalist hotel on the cliff above Ponta do Sol seafront.

The Vine (www.hotelthevine.com) One of Europe's finest design hotels in downtown Funchal.

Reid's Palace (www.belmond.com) Still traditionally Madeira's most illustrious hotel with a star-studded guest list.

Pestana Grand (www.pestana.com) Five-star affair located at the quiet end of the Hotel Zone at Ponta da Cruz.

Arriving in Madeira

....

Madeira Airport

➔ The **SAM Aerobus** (www.sam.pt; single/return €5/8) runs between the airport and Praia Formosa via the city centre and the Hotel Zone around 17 times a day, coinciding with flight arrivals and departures.

➔ SAM bus 113 stops at the airport on its way from Machico to Funchal city centre.

➜Prearrange a transfer with **Madeira Airport Transfers** (www.madeira-airport-transfers.com; 1-way trip €23). Online booking available.

Cruise Terminal

➜Funchal city centre is reachable on foot in around 15 minutes.

➜From the city centre, take **Horários do Funchal** (www.horariosdofunchal.pt) bus 01, 02 or 04 to the Hotel Zone.

➜Taxis wait near the terminal.

Porto Santo Airport

➜The only way to get from Porto Santo Airport to your hotel is by taxi. These wait at the terminal when flights are due.

Getting Around

Bus

☑ **Best for**...Most travel on Madeira.

Only a handful of buses originate or terminate anywhere else than Funchal. The following bus companies operate on Madeira:

Horários do Funchal (www.horariosdofunchal.pt) Operates all services in Funchal and selected routes to mountain destinations in Madeira's east.

Rodoeste (www.rodoeste.com.pt) Runs services to destinations west of Funchal.

SAM (www.sam.pt) Buses to all points east including the airport and Machico.

EACL (www.eacl.pt) Small company serving Caniço and Garajau.

Make sure you always keep your bus ticket to the end of the journey, whichever bus company you use, as inspections are very common.

Useful Services

➜**Horários do Funchal (urban routes)** 01, 02, 04 city centre–Hotel Zone; 48 Hotel Zone–Monte; 20/21 city centre–Monte; 22 city centre–Babosas.

➜**Horários do Funchal** (interurban routes) – 56/103 Santana via Ribeiro Frio; 81 Curral das Freiras; 113 Camacha.

➜**Rodoeste** 80 Porto Moniz; 139 Porto Moniz via São Vicente and Encumeada; 6 Encumeada; Ribeira Brava.

Bus Tickets

Most bus tickets on services operated by Madeira's bus companies are bought from the driver but there are exceptions. On Horários do Funchal city buses, you'll need a magnetic Giro card (€0.50), which you charge with cash at special machines on Funchal seafront. Buy the card from the machine, the driver or from Horários do Funchal sales points. Without a Giro a single journey in Funchal costs €1.95. With a Giro card charged with between two and nine journeys (*títulos*), the price is €1.25. A day ticket costs €4.60, a three-day ticket €11.80. There is nowhere in the Hotel Zone to charge up your Giro card, so make sure you have one journey left to get you back to the city centre.

SAM 23 Machico; 113 Baía D'Abra via Machico and Caniçal.

Departure Points

Funchal has no central bus station. The departure points for the various companies are as follows:

Horários do Funchal (urban routes) City buses leave from many points in Funchal seafront (Avenida do Mar).

Horários do Funchal (interurban routes) These services leave from a small bus station in Rua José da Silva in the Zona Velha.

Rodoeste The Rodoeste ticket office and main city-centre stop is outside the OPAN bakery cafe on Avenida do Mar. Many Rodoeste buses also stop at various points in the Hotel Zone.

SAM This company has its own station depot at Avenida Calouste Gulbenkian uphill and on the other side of the road from the Dolce Vita shopping centre. However most people choose to board at SAM's Avenida do Mar stop.

Money-Saving Tips

➡ Calculate how many journeys you are likely to make on Funchal's buses and charge up your Giro card accordingly.

➡ The free *Best of Madeira Guide* available at hotels and restaurants is packed with discount vouchers.

➡ Prebook your airport transfer and pay for it with PayPal.

➡ Use buses rather than taxis to access the levadas.

➡ Organise hikes yourself rather than going with a tour group.

➡ Never accept the first price drivers suggest when taking a taxi outside Funchal.

Car & Motorcycle

☑ **Best for**...Touring the island independently and accessing some levada walks.

➡ All international hire companies have airport and city-centre offices.

➡ You must be a confident driver to tackle roads outside Funchal, which can be extremely steep.

➡ There's ample parking everywhere on Madeira. Local car-hire companies:

Rodavante (www.rodavante.com)

Auto Jardim (www.carhiremadeira.net)

Guerin (www.guerin.pt)

Taxi

☑ **Best for**...Touring a lot of the island in a day without hiring a car, as well as accessing levada walks.

➡ Madeiran taxis are always yellow with a blue stripe along the side. The most common vehicles are Mercedes saloons and Mercedes minivans.

➡ Fares are €2.50 pick-up charge (€3 at night and weekends) plus €0.66 (€0.79) per kilometre. You might also pay for baggage.

➡ In Funchal fares are metered.

➡ Outside Funchal you can often haggle the unmetered price down a bit at quiet times.

➡ Many taxi owners/companies also run excursions and island tours. Expect to pay around €25 to €35 per person for a full day.

➡ Hotel receptions can always summon a trustworthy taxi for you.

➡ Some taxis tout for business at bus stops. Don't encourage this by accepting a ride.

Bicycle

☑ **Best for**...Getting around the Hotel Zone and Funchal city centre.

➡ Cycle hire is not widespread though there are a couple of places in the Hotel Zone that rent out bikes.

➡ **Freeride Madeira** (www. freeridemadeira.com; Hotel Porto Mare, Rua Simplício Passos de Gouveia 21, Funchal) rents out quality mountain bikes from €25 a day.

Boat

☑ **Best for**...Getting to Porto Santo and other islands.

➡ The only ferry service in the archipelago is **Porto**

Santo Line (☎291 210 300; www.portosantoline.pt; return €46.95-57.40), which runs to Porto Santo once a day.

➡ Other nonscheduled tour services operate to the Desertas Islands and out to sea for fishing and wildlife-spotting trips, including ones run by recommended operator **Ventura** (Map p34; ☎963 691 995; www.venturadomar. com; Funchal Marina).

Essential Information

Business Hours

☑ **Top Tip** All museums have at least one day when they remain closed. Most also have a short lunch break.

Smaller shops close on Sundays but malls and supermarkets are open normal hours. Standard opening hours:

Shops 9am to 7pm

Museums 10am to 12.30pm, 2pm to 6pm

Post Offices 8.30am to 8pm Monday to Friday, 9am to 1pm Saturday

Restaurants noon to 3pm, 6pm to 11pm

Electricity

220V/50Hz

Emergencies

General emergency number ☎112

Police ☎291 208 400

Fire ☎291 200 930

Medical emergency ☎291 204 480

Money

☑ **Top Tip** You'll need cash for bus and taxi fares.

➡ Madeira uses the euro (€).

➡ ATMs are widespread.

➡ Tipping is rarely expected.

Credit and debit cards re accepted by the vast ajority of businesses, ough cafes and small hops may only take ash.

ublic Holidays

ome national holidays ave been cancelled ntil 2019 as an austerity easure. It's not certain hether these will be einstated after that date. hey do not feature in the llowing list.

Portuguese and adeiran public holidays:

ew Year's Day
January

arnaval (Mon)
0 days before Easter
onday

aster March/April

iberation Day
5 April

abour Day 1 May

ational Day 10 June

ladeira Day 1 July

ssumption
August

unchal City Day
1 August

nmaculate Conception
December

hristmas Day
5 December

Safe Travel

☑ **Top Tip** Stay away from beaches and sea-fronts during storms – Atlantic waves can be huge and often swamp promenades.

➡ Madeira is one of the safest places on earth as far as crime is concerned.

➡ Flash floods and the resulting land slips and rock falls are the greatest dangers to visitors.

➡ Check with the tourist office if you are unsure if a hiking route is open.

➡ Stay away from any river where the water level is rising after heavy rain.

➡ Never pass a barrier on a hiking trail that prohibits walkers from continuing.

Telephone Services

Mobile Phones

➡ All EU mobiles work on Madeira and EU tariffs apply.

➡ Portuguese SIM cards are only good value if you are staying more than a couple of weeks.

➡ GSM signal coverage is surprisingly good, even in remote areas.

Phone Codes

➡ The international code for Portugal is 📞 +351.

Dos & Don'ts

➡ Smart casual attire may be expected in some upmarket restaurants and places of entertainment.

➡ Always allow locals with children to board buses first. If you are travelling with children, locals will do the same.

➡ Give up your seat on buses to the elderly and to children.

➡ Don't encourage taxis touting at bus stops by accepting rides.

➡ Do learn a few phrases of Portuguese – Madeirans are very polite and appreciate the odd *bom dia* (hello) and *obrigado* (thank you) from foreigners.

➡ All numbers on Madeira start with ☎291 followed by six digits.

➡ To call a Madeiran subscriber from abroad, dial ☎+351 291 XXX XXX.

Toilets

➡ Toilets are usually free, well-maintained and strategically located.

➡ Gentlemen's conveniences are often marked with the letter 'H' (*homens*), the ladies with an 'S' (*senhoras*).

Tourist Information

The main **turismo** (tourist office; Map p34; ☎291 211 902; www.visitmadeira.pt; Avenida Arriaga 16; ⊙9am-8pm Mon-Fri, 9am-3.30pm Sat & Sun) can field most questions though staff can be a bit flummoxed and visitor weary.

There are other branches at the airport, at the Centro Comercial Monumental, at the cruise terminal and in Curral das Freiras, Santana, Porto Moniz, Vila Baleira and Ribeira Brava.

Travellers with Disabilities

➡ Modern hotels in the Hotel Zone must have disabled facilities by law.

➡ Buses between the Hotel Zone and the city centre have disabled access.

➡ Outside Funchal things are not particularly wheelchair friendly.

➡ The cable car to Monte has disabled access.

➡ Some 2km of the Pico das Pedras to Queimadas trail has been made wheelchair accessible.

➡ **Accessible Portugal** (www.accessibleportugal. com) is a travel agency specialising in tours for travellers with disabilites in Portugal, including Madeira.

Visas

➡ As an autonomous region of Portugal, Madeira is part of the Schengen zone.

➡ EU nationals can stay indefinitely.

➡ All other nationals should check with their Portuguese embassy.

Language

Most sounds in Portuguese are also found in English. The exceptions are the nasal vowels (represented in our pronunciation guides by 'ng' after the vowel), pronounced as if you're trying to make the sound through your nose; and the strongly rolled *r* (represented by 'rr' in our pronunciation guides). Also note that the symbol 'zh' sounds like the 's' in 'pleasure'. Keeping these few points in mind and reading the pronunciation guides as if they were English, you'll be understood just fine. The stressed syllables are indicated with italics.

To enhance your trip with a phrasebook, visit **lonelyplanet.com**.

Basics

Hello.
Olá.   o·*laa*

Goodbye.
Adeus.   a·de·*oosh*

How are you?
Como está?   ko·moo shtaa

Fine, and you?
Bem, e você?   beng e vo·*se*

Please.
Por favor.   poor fa·*vor*

Thank you.
Obrigado. (m)   o·bree·*gaa*·doo
Obrigada. (f)   o·bree·*gaa*·da

Excuse me.
Faz favor.   faash fa·*vor*

Sorry.
Desculpe.   desh·*kool*·pe

Yes./No.
Sim./Não.   seeng/nowng

I don't understand.
Não entendo.   nowng eng·*teng*·doo

Do you speak English?
Fala inglês?   faa·la eeng·*glesh*

Eating & Drinking

..., please.   *..., por favor.*   ... poor fa·*vor*

A coffee   *Um café*   oong ka·fe

A table   *Uma mesa*   oo·ma me·za
  for two   *para duas*   pa·ra doo·ash
                   pessoas   pe·so·ash

Two beers   *Dois*   doysh
                   cervejas   ser·*ve*·zhash

I'm a vegetarian.
Eu sou   e·oo soh
vegetariano/   ve·zhe·a·ree·a·noo/
vegetariana. (m/f) ve·zhe·a·ree·a·na

Cheers!
Saúde!   sa·oo·de

That was delicious!
Isto estava   eesh·too shtaa·va
delicioso.   de·lee·see·o·zoo

The bill, please.
A conta, por favor. a kong·ta poor fa·*vor*

Shopping

I'd like to buy ...
Queria   ke·ree·a
comprar ...   kong·*praar* ...

I'm just looking.
Estou só a ver. shtoh so a ver

How much is it?
Quanto custa?   kwang·too koosh·ta

It's too expensive.
Está muito
caro.
shtaa *mweeng*·too
kaa·roo

Can you lower the price?
Pode baixar
o preço?
po·de bai·*shaar*
oo pre·soo

Emergencies

Help!
Socorro!
soo·ko·rroo

Call a doctor!
Chame um
médico!
shaa·me oong
me·dee·koo

Call the police!
Chame a
polícia!
shaa·me a
poo·*lee*·sya

I'm sick.
Estou doente.
shtoh doo·*eng*·te

I'm lost.
Estou perdido. (m)
Estou perdida. (f)
shtoh per·*dee*·doo
shtoh per·*dee*·da

Where's the toilet?
Onde é a casa de
banho?
ong·de e a *kaa*·za de
ba·nyoo

Time & Numbers

What time is it?
Que horas são?
kee o·rash sowng

It's (10) o'clock.
São (dez) horas.
sowng (desh) o·rash

Half past (10).
(Dez) e meia.
(desh) e *may*·a

morning	*manhã*	ma·*nyang*
afternoon	*tarde*	*taar*·de
evening	*noite*	*noy*·te
yesterday	*ontem*	*ong*·teng

today	*hoje*	o·zhe
tomorrow	*amanhã*	aa·ma·*nyang*

1	*um*	oong
2	*dois*	doysh
3	*três*	tresh
4	*quatro*	*kwaa*·troo
5	*cinco*	*seeng*·koo
6	*seis*	saysh
7	*sete*	*se*·te
8	*oito*	*oy*·too
9	*nove*	*no*·ve
10	*dez*	desh

Transport & Directions

Where's ...?
Onde é ...?
ong·de e ...

What's the address?
Qual é o
endereço?
kwaal e oo
eng·de·*re*·soo

Can you show me (on the map)?
Pode-me
mostrar
(no mapa)?
po·de·me
moosh·*traar*
(noo *maa*·pa)

When's the next bus?
Quando é que sai
o próximo
autocarro?
kwang·doo e ke sa
oo *pro*·see·moo
ow·to·*kaa*·rroo

I want to go to ...
Queria ir a ...
ke·*ree*·a eer a ...

Does it stop at ...?
Pára em ...?
paa·ra eng ...

Please stop here.
Por favor pare
aqui.
poor fa·*vor paa*·re
a·*kee*

Behind the Scenes

Send Us Your Feedback

We love to hear from travellers – your comments help make our books better. We read every word, and we guarantee that your feedback goes straight to the authors. Visit **lonelyplanet.com/contact** to submit your updates and suggestions.

Note: We may edit, reproduce and incorporate your comments in Lonely Planet products such as guidebooks, websites and digital products, so let us know if you don't want your comments reproduced or your name acknowledged. For a copy of our privacy policy visit lonelyplanet.com/privacy.

Marc's Thanks

Huge thanks go to parents-in-law Mykola and Vira for looking after the boys in Funchal; to Cath Ferreira for the excellent base in Ajuda, Carlos Pereira of History Tellers, everyone at Armazém do Mercado, Madeira Film Experience and Santa Maria Hostel, tourist office staff around Madeira and my wife Tanya.

Acknowledgments

Cover photograph: Port and harbour of Câmara de Lobos, eye35.pix/Alamy

Contents photograph: Câmara de Lobos, Juergen Sack/Getty Images

This Book

This 1st edition of Lonely Planet's *Madeira* guidebook was researched and written by Marc Di Duca. This guidebook was produced by the following:

Destination Editor
Lorna Parkes
Product Editors
Catherine Naghten,
Tracy Whitmey
Senior Cartographer
Anthony Phelan
Book Designers
Katherine Marsh,
Virginia Moreno,
Wendy Wright

Assisting Editors
Kate Evans, Rosie Nicholson
Cover Researcher
Campbell McKenzie
Thanks to Sasha Baskett,
Jo Cooke, Ryan Evans,
Andi Jones, Karyn Noble,
Diana Saengkham,
Angela Tinson, Tony
Wheeler, Amanda
Williamson

Index

See also separate subindexes for:

- ⊗ Eating p150
- 🍷 **Drinking p151**
- ☆ **Entertainment p151**
- 🔓 **Shopping p151**

A

accommodation 138-9
Aeroporto da Madeira 85
A-frame houses 76
ambulance 142
animals 87
Aquário da Madeira 75
area codes 143-4
Armazém do Mercado 64
arts 11, 67, 82-3
ATMs 142

B

Balcões 109
bathrooms 144
beaches 132
beer 126
Biblioteca de Culturas Estrangeiras 33
Bica da Cana 110
bicycle travel 142
bird-watching 95
Blandy's 135
boat travel 142
Boca da Encumeada 109-10
bolo de mel 40, 124
Borges 135
bus travel 140-1
business hours 142

Experiences 000
Map Pages **000**

C

Cabo Girão 101
Cais do Sardinha 123
Caldeirão Verde 95
Camacha Wicker Factory 11, 82-3
Câmara de Lobos 102, 103
Caniço 79
Caniço de Baixo 79
Capela do Corpo Santo 51
Capela dos Milagres 85
car travel 141
Carnaval 131
Casa da Luz Museu de Electricidade 57
Casa das Mudas 102
Casa Museu Colombo (Porto Santo) 114
Casa Museu Frederico de Freitas 36
cell phones 16, 143
Cemitério de São Martinho 33
Centro Ciência Viva 75
children, travel with 130
climate 138
Clube Naval do Funchal 31
coffee 62
Colombus, Christopher 114
Complexo Balnear Lido Galomar 132
Complexo Balnear Ponta Gorda 31

Convento de Santa Clara 37-8
Corrida 120
costs 16, 134, 140, 141
credit cards 143
Cristo Rei 85
Curral das Freiras 9, 106-7
currency 142
cycling 142

D

dangers 143
disabilities, travellers with 144
dolphin tours 129
door art 67
drinking 126, 135, *see also individual regions*, Drinking *subindex*
drives 12, 78-9
driving 141

E

East Funchal 48-67, **56**
  drinking & nightlife 62
  entertainment 64
  experiences 50-1, 52-3, 54-5, 57-9
  food 59-61
  itineraries 49
  shopping 64-7
  transport 49

east Madeira 12, 80-7, **8**
  itineraries 78-9, 81, **78**
  transport 81
electric-car tours 129
electricity 16, 142
emergencies 142
Encumeada Pass 121
entertainment *see individual regions*, Entertainment *subindex*
environment 87
espada 103, 124
espetada 124
Estádio dos Barreiros 33
etiquette 143
events 65, 131
explorers 41, 63, 114

F

fado music 44
Faial 79
fauna 87
ferry services 142
Festa da Flor 131
Festa de Nossa Senhora do Monte 131
Festival do Atlântico 131
festivals 65, 131
Fim do Ano 131
fire department 142
fishing industry 103

...ding 143
...a 87, 95
... dancing 65
...d 124-5, see also
  individual regions,
  Eating subindex
...taleza de
  Santiago 58
...taleza do Pico 38
...nco, Francisco 58
...e attractions 134
...nte Mar 12, 30-1, **30**
...ts 124
...chal 22-47, 48-
  ...67, see also East
  Funchal, West
  Funchal
...chal Marathon 131

...eries 128, see
  also individual
  galleries
...dens 136, see
  also individual
  gardens
...a 126
... 114
...tas e Centro do
  Vulcanismo 75

...sburgs, the 71
**...riques &
  Henriques 135**
...lights 8-11, 12-13
...ory
...olumbus,
  Christopher 114
...xplorers 41, 63
...absburgs, the 71
...vadas 90
...urs 129
...ansport 110
...days 143

I

IBTAM 58
**Igreja da Nossa
  Senhora 69**
**Igreja de
  São Bento 101-2**
**Igreja de São
  Martinho 33**
**Igreja do Bom
  Jesus 76**
Igreja do Socorro 59
Ilhéu do Lido 31
interior Madeira,
  see mountains of
  the interior
itineraries 14-15, 118-23,
  119, **121**, **123**, see
  also individual
  regions
  levadas 92-7

J

**Jardim de Santa
  Luzia 38**
**Jardim de São
  Martinho 33**
**Jardim do Almirante
  Reis 51**
Jardim Municipal 38
Jardim Panorâmico 31
**Jardins Botânicos da
  Madeira 10, 54-5**
Jardins do Palheiro 57

K

Karl I, Emperor of
  Austria 71

L

languages 16, 60, 145-6
levada tours 129
levadas 88-97
Lido 30
local life 12-13
Louro Parque 55

M

Machico 79, 86, 132
Machin, Robert 86
Madalena do Mar 133
**Madeira Film
  Experience 36**
Mata da Nazaré 33
**Mercado dos
  Lavradores 10, 52-3**
mobile phones 16, 143
money 16, 134, 141,
  142-3
Monte 9, 68-71, 79
**Monte Palace Tropical
  Gardens 70**
Morro do Furado 123
motorcycle travel 141
mountains of the
  interior 104-11, **108**
  itineraries 105
  transport 105
Museu CR7 36
Museu da Baleia 85
**Museu de Arte Sacra
  11, 26-7**
**Museu do
  Brinquedo 58**
**Museu Etnográfico
  da Madeira 101**
**Museu Photographia
  Vicentes 36-7**
museums 128, see
  also individual
  museums
music 65

N

nightlife 126, see also
  Drinking subindex
Ninho da Manta 118
Noite do Mercado 131
north coast 72-7, **74**
  itineraries 73
  transport 73
north coast road 77

O

opening hours 142

P

parks 136, see
  also individual
  parks
**Parque de Santa
  Catarina 38**
**Parque Temático da
  Madeira 75-6**
Paúl da Serra 111
Paúl do Mar 133
Pereira D'Oliveira 135
**Pico Castelo
  (Porto Santo) 114**
Pico das Torres 119
**Pico de Ana Ferreira
  (Porto Santo) 114**
**Pico do Arieiro 79,
  109, 118**
**Pico do Facho
  (Porto Santo) 114**
**Pico dos
  Barcelos 32**
**Pico Grande
  Escarpment 121**
Pico Ruivo 119
Piscinas Naturais 132
planning 16-17
Poiso 79
police 142
poncha 126
Ponta da Cruz 31
Ponta do Pargo 102
Ponta do Sol 133
Porta da Cruz 76
**Portela viewpoint
  (Porto Santo) 114**
**Porto Santo 10,
  112-15, 115**
**Porto Santo Golfe
  (Porto Santo) 114**
Portuguese language
  145-6

Praia da Calheta 132
Praia de Garajau 132
Praia de Machico 132
Praia do Arieiro 132
Praia Formosa 31, 132
public holidays 143

Q
Queimadas Forest
Park 95
Quinta da
Boa Vista 59
Quinta das Cruzes
Museum 9, 24-5
Quinta Magnólia
Gardens 33
Quinta Vigia 38

R
Ribeira Brava 133
Ribeira do Poço 121
Ribeiro Frio 79, 133
Ribeiro Frio Trout
Farm 110
Risco Waterfall 97
Ronaldo, Cristiano 36,
37, 39
Ronaldo statue 37

S
safety 143
Santa Cruz 79
Santana 76
São Martinho 12,
32-3, **32**
São Vicente 133
Sé (Cathedral) 11,
28-9
seafood 124
seahorse rocks 122
Serra de Água 133

Experiences 000
Map Pages 000

shopping 45, 127, see
also individual
regions, Shopping
subindex
swimming 132

T
taxis 141-2
Teleférico 51, 70
telephone services 16,
143-4
time 16
tipping 142
tobogganing 69
toilets 144
top experiences 8-11
tourist information 144
tours 129
transport 17, 110,
139-44, 140-4
Túnel do Pico do
Gato 118
tuk-tuk tours 129

U
Universo de Memórias
João Carlos
Abreu 36

V
vacations 143
villages 133
visas 144

W
walking tours 129
walks 118-23
Frente Mar 12,
30-1, **30**
levadas 92-3, 94,
96-7
São Martinho 12,
32-3, **32**
weather 138
websites 16, 138-9

West Funchal 22-47,
34-5
drinking &
nightlife 42-4
entertainment 44-5
experiences 24-5,
26-7, 36-8
food 40-2
itineraries 23, 30-1,
32-3, **30**, **32**
shopping 45-7
transport 23
west Madeira
98-103, **100**
itineraries 99
transport 99
whale-watching
tours 129
wicker weaving 82-3
wine 42, 135

Y
yacht tours 129

Z
Zona Velha 8, 50-1

⊗ Eating

A Central 86
A Confeitaria 41
Alto Monte 69
Armazém do Sal 41
Atlantis 86
Baiana (Porto Santo) 113
Boho Bistrô 40
Borda D'Agua 103
Cachelote 77
Cafe do Parque 69
Cantinho da Serra 76
Casa de Abrigo do
Poiso 111
Churrascaria
Santana 77

Convento das
Vinhas 103
Doca do Cavacas 31
Estrela do Norte 76
Ferro Velho 77
Gavião Novo 59
Hamburgueria do
Mercado 60
Il Gallo d'Oro 40
Jardim Botânicos da
Madeira Snack
Bar 55
La Perla 86
Leque 27
Londres 41-2
Macaronésia 53
Maré Alta 86
Mercado Velho 86
Muralha 103
O Celeiro 40
O Relógio 83
Oficina 60
Pé na Água
(Porto Santo) 113
Prince Charles Snack
Bar 25
Quebra Mar 77
Quinta da Serra 102
Quinta do Furão 76
Reid's Hotel Tea
Terrace 33
Restaurante Ribeiro
Frio 111
Restaurantes dos
Combatentes 40
Riso 60
Sabores do Curral 11
Santa Maria 60
Tasca Literária 61
Teahouse 25
Vale das Freiras 111
Venda da Donna
Maria 61
Vila da Carne 103
Vila do Peixe 102

Drinking

Vintage Bar 64
reirinha Cafe 62
rhouse 44
e do Museu 43
e do Teatro 42
acabana 42
a de Chá 44
rcearia da Poncha 62
i Eco Bar 43
de Canela 62
ha D'Águia 43-4
nce Albert Pub 42

Santa Maria Gin Bar 62
Venda Velha 62
Vespas 42

Entertainment

Arsenio's 64
Casino da Madeira 44
Sabor e Fado 64
Scat Funchal
    Jazz Club 44-5
Teatro Baltazar
    Dias 45

Shopping

Armazém do
    Mercado 64
Artecouro 47
Bordal 67
Casa do Turista 45
Dolce Vita 46
Fabrica de Chapeus
    de Santa Maria 67
Fábrica Ribeiro
    Sêco 46
Fabrica Santo
    Antonio 46

Livraria Esperança 45
Madeira Lovers 66
Madeira Shopping 46
Madeira Tradicional 66
Mercado dos
    Lavradores 52-3
Mercearia Dona
    Mécia 47
O Bordão 46
Patrício &
    Gouveia 64
Saudade Madeira 46

Our Writer

Marc Di Duca

Author and updater of several guides to Madeira, Marc was thrilled to hear that the island of eternal spring was to get the Lonely Planet treatment. And why? Because Madeira is without doubt his favourite place on earth, bar none! Over five prolonged trips Marc has visited every hidden corner of this subtropical paradise, both as a travel guide author and as a keen hiker, father of two and avid custard tart eater. When not sampling *pastel de nata* in every single Madeiran cafe, counting scabbard fish at the Mercado dos Lavradores or being soundly thrashed at football by the Ronaldo-esque kids of Funchal, Marc can be found in Sandwich, Kent, where he lives with his Ukrainian wife and their two sons.

Published by Lonely Planet Publications Pty Ltd
ABN 36 005 607 983
1st edition – December 2015
ISBN 978 1 74360 710 7
© Lonely Planet 2015   Photographs © as indicated 2015
10 9 8 7 6 5 4 3 2 1
Printed in China